TANK BATTLES
OF
WORLD WAR I

BRYAN COOPER

Pen & Sword
MILITARY

First published in Great Britain in 1974 by Ian Allan Ltd
Reprinted in 2014 and reprinted in this format in 2022 by
PEN & SWORD MILITARY
An imprint of
Pen & Sword Books Ltd
47 Church Street
Barnsley, South Yorkshire
S70 2AS

ISBN 978 1 39901 986 6

A CIP catalogue record for this book is
available from the British Library

Printed and bound in England by CPI Group (UK) Ltd, Croydon, CR0 4YY

Pen & Sword Books Ltd incorporates the Imprints of Aviation, Atlas,
Family History, Fiction, Maritime, Military, Discovery, Politics, History,
Archaeology, Select, Wharncliffe Local History, Wharncliffe True Crime,
Military Classics, Wharncliffe Transport, Leo Cooper, The Praetorian Press,
Remember When, Seaforth Publishing and Frontline Publishing

For a complete list of Pen & Sword titles please contact
PEN & SWORD BOOKS LIMITED
47 Church Street, Barnsley, South Yorkshire, S70 2AS, England
E-mail: enquiries@pen-and-sword.co.uk
Website: www.pen-and-sword.co.uk

TANK BATTLES
OF
WORLD WAR I

Other books by Bryan Cooper

*The Ironclads of Cambrai**
North Sea Oil – The Great Gamble
Battle of the Torpedo Boats
The Buccaneers
PT Boats
Alaska – The Last Frontier
A History of Fighter Aircraft
A History of Bomber Aircraft
*The E-Boat Threat**
The Adventure of North Sea Oil
*The War of the Gunboats**

NOVELS
Stones of Evil
The Wildcatters

*Denotes titles in print with Pen & Sword Books Ltd

Contents

The Author and publisher
are indebted to the
Imperial War Museum
for supplying the photographs
used in this book.

CHAPTER ONE

Birth of the Tank

It would be very difficult to imagine a war today being fought without the use of tanks. They are vital to the armies of even the smallest nations, the spearhead force of any land attack, in many ways the epitome of modern warfare. Assuming a more or less even balance in other factors such as air power, an army without tanks would have little chance of success.

But that was precisely the situation which occurred in World War I. The tank did not exist before the war began. It was invented by the British and used for the first time in 1916, one of the most devastating weapons ever to be introduced during a war. For two years the British and the French, who to a lesser degree also developed tanks of their own, had a monopoly in the use of this new weapon. By the time the Germans came to realise the enormous potential of the tank and frantically started to build their own, it was far too late. Only 15 German tanks ever came into action, as against over 4,000 British and French. In the final battles of 1918, tanks were the most decisive single factor in securing victory for the Allies.

With such a clear superiority, it might be wondered why tanks did not make a greater impact earlier than they did. They would have done had it not been for the extraordinary reluctance to accept them on the part of tradition-bound military commanders who lacked the imagination to see that the nature of war had completely changed. It was only by the dogged persistence of a few far-sighted individuals that tanks became available at all to the British Army on the Western Front. Even then they were badly misused. The powerful element of surprise that could have been achieved by the introduction of such a secret weapon was dissipated by minor and inconclusive actions in the mud of Flanders. A very real chance of ending the war earlier was thrown away by generals who still pinned their faith on the cavalry and dreamed of a great sabre-drawn charge through the German lines, a costly dream that required 80,000 tons of fodder a month for the 400,000 horses maintained by the British Army.

The Germans also clung to outmoded ideas, although this was less apparent in the early years of the war. Their greatest weapons were the machine gun, largely responsible for the stalemate that existed on the Western Front after the race for the coast had become drawn, and long range artillery bombardment for which they possessed a clear superiority in munitions over the British and French. Their own answer to counter bombardment by the Allies was to dig in, creating in the Hindenburg Line the greatest defensive system the world had ever seen, four miles wide in places with huge electrically-lit and heated dugouts where a company of men could lie secure 40ft below ground until the shelling was over. They would then emerge and from their concrete machine gun posts annihilate the attacking infantry who were trying to claw a way through the massed barbed wire. Hundreds of thousands of unprotected troops were mown down in such suicidal attacks.

While the Allied commanders fought their reckless war of attrition, a policy of despair that sought nothing more than to wear the enemy down by swapping life for life, the Germans had reason to be confident that their defences were impregnable. Only when tanks appeared, armoured against the machine gun, able to crush through the barbed wire to make way for and give cover to the following infantry, were these mighty defences broken. The very trenches that had given such protection before became death traps as the tanks cruised up and down pouring a hail of fire into them.

The reasons for the stalemate on the Western Front were not surprising. There had not been a war between the major powers since 1871 and most people had no awareness of what war was like, still less the imagination to see how it might have developed from the time of the Franco-Prussian war. Each of the European nations which mobilised—and no less than six million men were sent into the first battles—was certain it was doing so in its own defence. Even the German advance through Belgium was part of a defensive deployment which became inevitable once Russia refused to demobilise. What had begun as a game of diplomatic bluff got so out of hand that no one knew how to stop it. But there was no shortage of slogans to sustain the momentum. The British, protected from invasion by the Grand Fleet and confident that it would all be over in a few months, decided it was going to be a 'war to end war', to make the 'world safe for democracy', themes that were later taken up by other countries. What very few realised, least of all the elderly commanders who owed their promotion to politics rather than ability, was the effect that modern technology would have, particularly in transportation.

The paradox lay in the fact that although the age was still that of the horse and none of the armies had mechanical transport to begin with, it was still possible to bring troops into battle very quickly by means of the railway. Trains could speed reinforcements to any part of the Front where they were required. Once they reached the railhead however, the troops had to slog it on foot, moving no faster than in any century past and indeed sometimes much slower, such were the numbers involved. Before an attacking side could break through on foot, the defenders could more rapidly bring up reinforcements to plug the gap. The defence was mechanised whereas the attack was not, therefore the defence was always stronger. But the military authorities were all agreed that the only effective means of waging war was to attack. Thus occurred the appalling casualties as men were thrown without protection against strongly defended positions. Even when they did succeed in breaking through, they were always beaten back by a rapid build-up of reinforcements. This was the case time and time again until something could be found to change the pattern. And that something was the tank.

There was nothing new in the concept of combat vehicles. The use of chariots and wheeled battle wagons goes back to the dawn of recorded history. The fast two wheeled chariots of the Assyrians, used more as fighting platforms than as weapon carriers, dominated wars between the years 1100 to 670 BC. The armoured cavalry of the Middle Ages was a form of such warfare until its power was ended, first by the well organised used of the longbow and then the invention of gunpowder and the musket. From that point on much of the mobility was taken out of warfare until, ironically, it was reintroduced by tanks. The analogy goes even further with the development of the two tanks which played the biggest part in the battles of 1918, the heavy Mark V and the light Whippet, each with a distinctive role corresponding to that of heavy and light cavalry. The only difference was that now, instead of the thunder of horses' hooves, the ground trembled with a new kind of thunder as fire belching monsters of iron and steel lumbered forward on grating tracks. But the affinity for horses was deeply embedded in the British character and even after the war, cavalrymen were ever ready to disparage the tank in defence of the horse. This attitude was prevalent up to the beginning of the Second World War in fact, gravely affecting the much needed modernisation of the British Army. The Germans made no such mistake. Having learned a painful lesson in 1918, they based the development of their new army on the tank, with devastating results in the early years of the war when their Panzer divisions swept all before them in Europe and the steppes of Russia.

From as early as the fourteenth century, various ideas for mechanical combat vehicles had been put forward. (One of the most practical designs was by Leonardo da Vinci, involving a shallow metal bowl with slits cut in the bottom to take the wheels which were to be hand-cranked by eight men through a system of gears.) During succeeding centuries attempts were made to harness this idea, but it was not until the advent of steam power that a means was found of driving such a vehicle. An assault vehicle was invented at the time of the Crimea War by James Cowan, a formidable machine similar to the da Vinci design with cannons fitted through loopholes in the sides and rotating scythes on the outside framework for mowing down the infantry. But Lord Palmerston rejected it as too brutal for civilised use.

It was the invention of the internal combustion engine in 1885, providing an economic mobile propulsion unit, that ultimately made possible the development of modern armoured fighting vehicles. An experimental armoured car was built by Frederick Simms and exhibited at Crystal Palace in 1902. Two machine guns were mounted in the turret and the driver steered with the aid of a periscope. The vehicle was not a big success because of its weight and low power, and this and other designs which followed were handicapped by the fact they could be used only on roads. They could not cross rough country and therefore offered no alternative to cavalry in battle.

But an answer even to this problem was in sight. Soon after the turn of the century, chain tracks had been developed for use on tractors, mainly steam-driven in those days. The firm of Richard Hornsby & Sons was responsible for much of this work and in 1908 the War Office bought one of their tracked vehicles for experimental purposes. Interest in Britain waned however, although Hornsby and others continued their research. Eventually Hornsby sold the American and Canadian patent rights to the Holt Caterpillar Company of New York. That company went ahead with further development work on tracks and by 1914 they were being used extensively on farm vehicles in the United States. It was not until after the war that tractors became popular in Britain, as a direct result of how effective tanks had proved themselves at the Front.

These two developments, the internal combustion engine and chain tracks, provided the main ingredients with which to make a tank. And the possibility was indeed seen by a number of people. In 1908, a Major Donoghue had suggested that a gun could be mounted on a Hornsby tractor, protected by armour. In 1912, an Australian called E. L. de Mole filed a design for an armoured fighting vehicle that was surprisingly similar to those which eventually went into service. It was in fact superior in many respects, par-ticularly its steering which was to be achieved by 'bowing' the tracks, a device ten years ahead of its time. But these and other ideas were pigeonholed and forgotten by an indifferent War Office. There was no interest in mechanical vehicles among cavalry indoctrinated commanders. Those closer to the Front were less hidebound however. During the first month or so of the conflict, as the Germans advanced across Belgium and then turned southwards through France in accordance with their prearranged plan and the French followed their own offensive plan by attacking the German fortifications in Lorraine, there was a real war of movement on the old European pattern. It was the only time this occurred before the initial impetus ran down and four years of deadlocked trench warfare followed. But it gave time for some interesting new ideas to be tried out.

The bulk of the British Expeditionary Force of 1914 had been sent to join up with the left flank of the French Army. This was of little help to beleaguered Belgium which was the ostensible reason for Britain entering the war but the British had their own set plan, prepared like those of Germany and France some years before the war with more concern for theory than actuality and the War Office insisted that no other course was possible. It was the rigidity of this kind of thinking that was largely responsible for setting in motion the tragic and irreversible sequence of events which followed, once the politicians had been cornered by their own miscalculations. Thus from the very start the British Army became embedded with the French on the Western Front and British policy lost much of its freedom of action. However, in an attempt to create a naval diversion, a small force of marines was sent to Ostend at the end of August by Winston Churchill, then First Sea Lord and ever ready to try something different. Supporting them was a squadron of the Royal Naval

Air Service under the command of a fiery and unconventional naval officer, Commander C. R. Samson. In the event the diversion did not prove possible and the marines were recalled after only three days. The squadron was supposed to return as well but this did not suit Samson. Using a Channel fog as an excuse he landed his ten aircraft in Dunkirk and managed to get permission to remain there for the purpose of supporting the French and bombing Zeppelin bases in Germany where airships were being built in preparation for raiding London.

In order to set up advanced air bases inland and to pick up any pilots forced to crash land in the countryside, the squadron was equipped with Rolls Royce cars, armed with machine guns. In the open warfare of that time they often came into conflict with enemy infantry patrols. To provide some protection for the crews, Samson hit on the idea of hanging boiler plates to the sides of the cars, improvised at a local steel works. So successful was this device that Rolls Royce, at the request of Commodore Murray Sueter who was in command of the Royal Naval Air Service at the Admiralty, began fitting proper armour-plate to the cars they were making for the Service. Later they extended the armour plate over the top to give complete protection and adding a revolving gun turret. These armoured cars, the first ever to be used in war, played an active part in support of the British infantry during the struggle for Ypres at the end of October, operating as the 'Dunkirk Armoured Car Force'. As long as the roads remained open they dominated the actions in which they fought. But once the conflict bogged down into the stalemate of trench warfare, there seemed to be no further use for them. By the end of 1914, they had all been shipped back to England.

There the matter might have rested had it not been for the determination of a few men of vision who saw the need for some kind of fighting machine that could cross trenches and so end the deadlock that had been reached. One of these was Lieutenant-Colonel Ernest Swinton who at that time was an official observer at General Headquarters, writing reports for the Press under the pen name of 'Eyewitness'. He had seen the armoured cars in action and been impressed by their capabilities. Also, it so happened that some years before the war he had received a report on the Hornsby tracks tested by the War Office. He put two and two together and suggested to Lieutenant-Colonel Maurice Hankey, Secretary of the Committee of Imperial Defence, that if the armoured cars could be fitted with tracks instead of wheels, they might well suit that need. Hankey put the idea forward but could arouse little interest in it, particularly at the War Office where Lord Kitchener considered such vehicles would too easily be shot up by guns. It was only when Churchill saw Hankey's memorandum on the subject and enlisted the support of the Prime Minister, Mr Asquith, that the War Office was compelled at least to examine the possibilities. Churchill was well aware of the success of Samson's armoured cars in Dunkirk and had been thinking along similar lines himself of the need to overcome the impasse of trench warfare.

With extreme reluctance the War Office conducted a trial at Shoeburyness

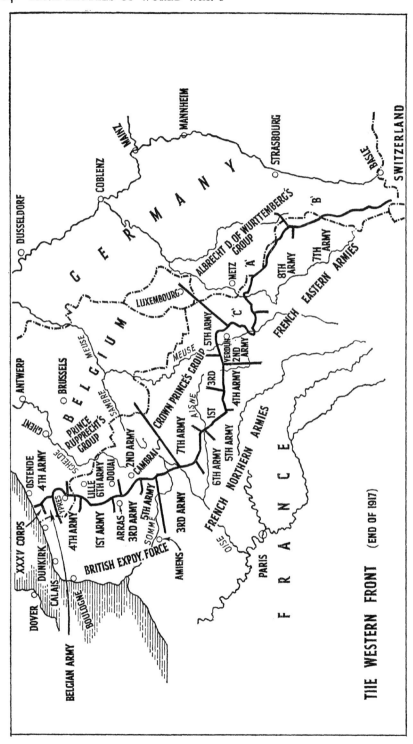

THE WESTERN FRONT   (END OF 1917)

in February 1915 with a Holt Caterpillar tractor previously brought over from the United States. The ground was waterlogged due to constant rain and not surprisingly, although the tractor succeeded in breaking through the barbed wire entanglements set up, it became stuck in the mud while trying to cross the prepared trenches. The fact that it was towing a heavy truck laden with sandbags, which was supposed to represent the weight of armour and armament, did not help. This impossible test convinced the delegation of high ranking officers present that they were right in their previous assessment that the idea was impractical.

But Churchill was not prepared to give up so easily. He took the initiative on behalf of the Navy and set up a Landship Committee at the Admiralty to look into ways of developing the idea. Following the failure of the Allied offensives in the spring of 1915 and prompted by demands from General Headquarters in France that a solution be found to the problem of trench warfare, the War Office at last began to show an interest and the Committee became a joint naval and military affair. But it was fitting, however curious to the uninitiated, that the first tanks to come into service were designed as 'His Majesty's Landships'—HMLS.

The task of building an experimental armoured vehicle was given to William Foster & Company of Lincoln. William Tritton, managing director of the firm, and Lieutenant Walter Wilson, a naval officer who was later transferred to the Army with rank of major, were the two men most responsible for the design. The prototype, named 'Little Willie', was little more than a mock-up, using whatever parts happened to be handy. It had a simple rectangular body of boiler plate, resting on tractor type tracks, and driven by a 105hp Daimler engine which gave a speed of about two miles an hour. Steering was achieved by throwing one or other of the tracks out of gear and a pair of tail wheels were towed behind to make the machine more stable. Trials were held in September 1915 but the two men were already working on new designs. Wilson in particular had hit on the revolutionary idea of taking the tracks right round a body of rhomboid shape, pointed at the top front and sloping down at the back. It was obviously the better design and everything else was dropped to concentrate on that. It was to become the basic shape of tanks for the rest of the war and indeed for some years afterwards.

'Big Willie' as it was called when given its initial trials in January 1916 was the first real tank. It was a remarkable vehicle, 31ft 3in long, 13ft 8in wide and 8ft high, with a total laden weight of 28tons. The tail wheels were still retained at the back, kept in contact with the ground by springs. Two 6pdr guns were mounted in large sponsons sticking out from each side of the hull. On the top were two fixed turrets, at front and rear. In the front turret there was room for the commander and the driver, sitting side by side, with a machine gun between them. There was another machine gun in the rear turret and semaphore arms on the outside which was the only means of communicating from one vehicle to another. There were four doors, one at the rear of the hull, a manhole on top, and one at the back of each sponson. The total crew numbered eight, the others being four gunners and two gearsmen. The engine was a 105hp Daimler giving a top speed of about 3·5mph. The armour was between 6mm and 12mm thick, reckoned to be sufficient to provide protection against a reverse bullet fired at ten yards, a standard measurement since the discovery a short while before that a bullet's armour piercing qualities were greater if it was reversed so that the lead core was driven on after the hard outer casing had been stopped.

During trials before increasingly distinguished audiences, including Lloyd George, Balfour, Lord Kitchener, and finally the King himself who rode in the tank, 'Big Willie' performed admirably. It climbed a parapet 4ft 6in high and crossed a trench 5ft wide, which was the official test, then went on to tackle an obstacle course consisting of prepared dugouts, shell craters, barbed wire entanglements, and a stream with sloping marshy edges. But even so, not everyone was enthusiastic. Lord Kitchener spoke of the machine as a 'pretty mechanical toy' and considered that the war would never be won by such vehicles.

It was this kind of attitude that had also deprived the British infantry of much needed machine guns. No more than two were allowed for each battalion because army commanders like Sir John French and Sir Douglas Haig felt they were overrated weapons and that in any case if battalions had too many, they might come to rely on them too much and show less inclination to 'go over the top' with fixed bayonets.

The dedicated band of pioneers who had made the tank possible, including Churchill, Swinton, Murray Sueter and Albert Stern who was secretary of the Landships Committee, saw that large numbers would be required to make a decisive impact during an offensive. They hoped for an order of hundreds, if not thousands, of the 'Big Willie' prototype which was officially designated as the Mark I. When the War Office finally made its decision, the order was for only 40. It took much argument and the direct intervention of Lloyd George, who was more impressed by what he had seen than the professional soldiers, to increase this order to 150. Kitchener's casual remark was a chilling augur for the future of tanks at the hands of the military establishment.

CHAPTER TWO

Preparing for Battle

The tank was developed with the utmost secrecy. Its very name was chosen so as not to reveal its true purpose. 'Landship' or 'landcruiser', as originally suggested, would have given too much away. On the other hand, its name had to be roughly consistent with its shape when seen under tarpaulin covers during transit by rail. Such terms as 'cistern', 'container' and 'reservoir' were considered before 'tank' was agreed upon as being suitably ambiguous. Apart from the actual vehicle, a name also had to be found for this new branch of the Army. It was first called the Tank Department but this again was felt to be too revealing and the name was changed to the Armoured Car Section of the Motor Machine Gun Service and then to the Heavy Section, Machine Gun Corps. Not until June 1917 did the new force become the Tank Corps, with the prefix Royal added after the war when the decision was made to retain it as a permanent part of the British Army.

The Germans knew nothing of the new weapon but ironically, they could have invented the tank before the British. As early as 1912 a certain Mr Steiner, who was Holt's representative in Austria, had tried to interest the military authorities in tracked petrol driven vehicles. The Austro-Hungarian army was interested but the German General Staff rejected them as having no importance for military purposes. It was an attitude with which many in the British War Office would have agreed.

It was envisaged from the outset that the tanks would work in pairs. One carrying the two 6pdr naval guns was to be supported by another armed only with machine guns to give protection in the event of a charge by enemy infantrymen. These were known respectively as 'male' and 'female' tanks. The 'females' carried two Vickers machine guns in each sponson, capable of shooting 1,200 rounds a minute on each side, in addition to the two machine guns in the front and rear turrets with which the 'males' were also armed.

While work began on building the first Mark I tanks, experiments were carried out on the design and construction of a more advanced vehicle which would, amongst other improvements, be proof against field gun shells as well as bullets. In the meantime, a search was made for volunteers to serve in the new force. Since no one could be told beforehand what it was all about, there was no rush of recruits. The name of the first base camp was hardly inviting; the one chosen was Siberia Camp near Bisley. But gradually, from March 1916 onwards, the numbers were built up, many of the officers and men coming from the Armoured Car Division of the Royal Naval Air Service.

There were no tanks available for training at first and when a few Mark I vehicles did begin to arrive at the end of May, it was not before the wildest rumours had spread throughout the camp as to what the new weapon could do—from climbing trees to swimming in the water.

One of the earliest recruits was Frederick L. Keyworth who served in the 9th Battalion and was awarded the Military Medal shortly before the end of the war. He later emigrated to the United States and became an American citizen. He wrote of his experiences:

"Training was very thorough. I first had to learn all the different parts of a tank. Then the next operation was the driving. The greater part of the camp was made to resemble the actual battlefield with trenches, shellholes, dugouts and mine craters. These I had to drive the tank over. One of the hardest parts of training was a sunken road with 6ft walls on each side and at the end a rightangled turn with about 3in clearance on either side. It was very hard to negotiate but it could be done by steering the tank round the corner inch by inch. After that procedure we went on to the battlefield which had to be negotiated without bogging down. Then came open ground where there were dummy men in the form of stuffed clothing made to represent wounded soldiers. They were strewn all over the field and we had to drive the tank around so as not to go over any of them. A number of posts were scattered around and we had to drive through these as well without knocking them over. Then we had to learn how to operate the Vickers machine guns and the Hotchkiss 6pdr."

The latter was a problem for there was no firing range available for practice. An attempt to use the Bisley rifle range, firing unfilled shell, was very quickly stopped by the War Office. The Royal Navy came to the rescue by offering their own facilities, and Keyworth was one of the first ten sent to the Naval gunnery school at Whale Island, Portsmouth.

"There we were temporarily transferred to the Navy. It was winter and we went to sea on a destroyer. Its action was supposed to represent the rolling and pitching of a tank. It was so rough at sea that when it was our turn to fire at a target towed by another ship they had to strap us to the gun.

"After ten days with the Navy we returned to our battalion. Each morning for a period of three months we went into a large shed, on the floor of which there was a model of a certain sector of France which we had to memorise so that when we got to France we would recognise the area.

"We never went near that sector all the time we were in France."

But even the makeshift training at Bisley was better than that which later took place in France after a Western Front headquarters had been established at Bermicourt, a small village on the road from Montreuil to Arras. A 'tanko-drome' training area was set up in a large field, but as very few tanks were available for instruction purposes, dummy ones were provided. These were described by Major W. H. L. Watson who later took command of a company of tanks.

"Imagine a large box of canvas stretched on a wooden frame, open at the top and bottom, about 6ft high, 8ft long and 5ft wide. Little slits were made in the canvas to represent the loopholes of a tank. Six men carried each dummy, lifting it by the crosspieces of the framework. For our sins we were issued with eight of these abominations.

"We started with a crew of officers to encourage the men, and the first dummy tank waddled out of the gate. It was immediately surrounded by a mob of cheering children, who thought it was an imitation dragon or something out of a circus. It was led away from the road to avoid hurting the feelings of the crew and to safeguard the ears and morals of the children. After colliding with the corner of a house, it endeavoured to walk down the side of a railway cutting. Nobody was hurt but a fresh crew was necessary. It regained the road when a small man in the middle, who had not been able to see anything, stumbled and fell. The dummy tank was sent back to the carpenters for repairs.

"We persevered with those dummy tanks. The men hated them. They were heavy, awkward, and produced much childish laughter. In another company, a crew walked over a steep place and a man broke his leg. The dummies became less and less mobile. The signallers practised from them and they were used by the visual training experts. One company commander mounted them on wagons drawn by mules. The crews were tucked in with their Lewis guns and each contraption, a cross between a fire engine and a triumphal car in the Lord Mayor's Show, would gallop past targets which the gunners would recklessly endeavour to hit.

"Eventually, and not entirely by accident, the dummies were broken up and the canvas and wood used for other purposes."

As more tanks began to arrive, the crews were able to train with the real thing. For many of the recruits it was their first sight of a tank and one can imagine their curiosity as the side doors were opened and they crawled inside. Such an experience was described by Richard Haig.

"We looked around the little chamber with eager curiosity. Our first thought was that seven men and an officer could never do any work in such a confined space. Eight of us were at present jammed in here but we were standing still. When it came to going into action and moving around inside the tank, it would be impossible. There was no room even to pass one another, so we thought. In front are two stiff seats, one for the officer and one for the driver. Two narrow slits serve as portholes through which we looked ahead. In front of the officer is a mapboard and gunmounting. Down the middle of the tank is the powerful petrol engine, part of it covered with a hood, and along each side a narrow passage along which a man can slide from the officer's and driver's seat back to the mechanism at the rear. There are four gun turrets, two each side, and also a place for a gun in the rear. Along the steel walls are numberless ingenious little cupboards in which stores and ammunition cases are stacked high. Every bit of space is utilised. Electric bulbs light the interior. Beside the driver are the engine levers. Behind the engine are the secondary gears by which the machine is turned in any direction. All action inside is directed by signals, for when the tank moves the noise is such as to drown a man's voice."

Steering was a team effort both laborious and complicated. Two gearsmen operated the gears on each track and both had to be shifted every time a change of direction was required. One would be put into high or low while the other, on the side to which it was intended to turn, was put into neutral. The driver would lock the differential and accelerate, the commander applied brakes to the neutral track, and the tank would swivel round until facing the intended direction. Then the whole process would have to be repeated in reverse to allow the vehicle to trundle forwards until the direction had to be altered yet again. Four men were required to drive a tank, leaving the other four to fire the guns. Because of the noise, the driver had to bang on the engine cover to attract the attention of the gearsmen and signal instructions with his fingers in accordance with a prearranged code. Another method of steering the Mark I was by means of the tail wheels. These could be turned like the rudder of a boat by a steering wheel from which cables ran back to the wheels. Countless problems were encountered due to stretching or slipping cables and none of the later models from the end of 1916 were fitted with tail wheels.

A major weakness of the Mark I was the fact that no silencer was provided for the engine. Consequently noise, sparks and even flames came from the open exhaust pipes passing through the roof of the tank, causing sickness and even asphyxiation. Some crews fitted ingenious silencers of their own, made from oil drums, or even covered the exhaust pipes with clay or mud. Improvements were made in the later models which came into use during the war— the Mark IV, the Mark V, and the Whippet—but none of the tanks were exactly comfortable. They were unsprung, badly ventilated, hot and fume-ridden, and so noisy that speech was impossible. Broken eardrums were not at all uncommon. Most of the interior was taken up by the large petrol engine so there was very little space for the crew to move about in as they struggled with the steering gears and looked for elusive targets through tiny peepholes in the armourplate which gave only limited arcs of view. While riding across rough, shell-cratered country, crews would be thrown from side to side as if weathering a stormy sea, often burning their flesh on hot parts of the engine. The men would have preferred to wear as little clothing as possible but they had to remain covered, including a cumbersome leather helmet and a mask of fine steel wire over the face, as protection against tiny particles of hot metal which were thrown off when the armour was struck by enemy projectiles.

Many men were continually sick and all suffered from headaches and singing noises in the ears which, according to medical reports, sometimes lasted for as long as 48 hours after an action. It was reckoned that three hours in a tank made a man unfit for duty for at least two and up to seven days afterwards. The heat from the engine, the choking petrol fumes and the smoke from the guns caused symptoms ranging from giddiness and palpitations to utter collapse, convulsions, and even mania. These were naturally aggravated when the enemy used gas and respirators had to be worn. A damaged exhaust could easily asphyxiate an entire crew with sometimes fatal consequences. Mental confusion was common, when men would sit and stare in front of them and merely repeat orders without carrying them out. Defects in ventilation led to chronic cases of carbon monoxide poisoning.

Apart from the sheer miseries involved, the greatest fear when a tank went into battle was of being burned, which could easily happen if the petrol tanks were set on fire. This might be caused by a direct hit from shellfire. There were, however, occasions when tanks went up in flames simply through sparks from bullet splash entering through the peepholes or even a red hot exhaust pipe igniting the air inside the tank after it had become saturated with petrol fumes. On the Mark I petrol was carried inside the cabin in two containers, one by the driver and the other by the commander, each holding 45 gallons. Apart from the ease with which the containers could be pierced by splinters, on more than one occasion blazing petrol leaked on to the ammunition racks and penetrated the 6pdr cartridge cases, setting fire to the cordite.

In spite of all this, the morale of the tank crews remained high. At least they were protected from the remorseless machine gun fire of the Germans, unlike the infantry, and although a direct hit from artillery fire would invariably put a tank out of action, for a long or short period depending on where it was hit, this was not necessarily disastrous for the crew if a fire could be prevented. In fact, direct hits caused remarkably few casualties among the crews. When during one action eight tanks were knocked out by shellfire, only one crew member was slightly wounded.

Something of the spirit of the tankmen was described by Sergeant Littledale, one of the first recruits to the new force.

"There is not one of us who will ever forget his first ride—the crawling in at the sides, the discovery that the height did not permit a man of medium stature to stand erect, the sudden starting of the engine, the roar of it all when the throttle opened, the jolt forward and the sliding through the mud that followed, until at last we came to the 'jump' which had been prepared. Then came the forward motion which suddenly threw us off our feet and caused us to stretch trusting hands towards the nearest object—usually, at first, a hot pipe through which the water from the cylinder jacket flowed to the radiator. So, down and down and down, the throttle almost closed, the engine just ticking over, until at last the bottom was reached, and as the power was turned full on, the tank raised herself to the incline, like a ship rising on a wave, and we were all jolted the other way, only to clutch again frantically for things which were hot and burned, until at last with a swing over the top we gained level ground. And in that moment we discovered that the trenches and the mud and the rain and the shells and the daily curse of bully beef had not killed everything within for there came to us a thrill of happiness in that we were to sail over stranger seas than man had ever crossed and set out on a great adventure."

The time was rapidly approaching for the tanks to see their first action.

While training of the crews went ahead in the spring and summer of 1916, Colonel Swinton, fittingly in command of the new force, had been giving thought as to how the tanks could best be used. In a lengthy memorandum on the employment of tanks, which contained a remarkable forecast of the tactics ultimately employed, he stressed the advantages of the tank such as its ability to crush barbed wire, cross trenches, and roll over enemy machine-gun emplacements which were the main scourge of the infantry, the reason for the appalling casualty rate on the Western Front. The chief weakness of tanks on the other hand, their vulnerability to artillery fire, was not much of a problem to the infantry as long as they could get near enough to deal with the field gun batteries. Each force, tanks and infantry, could therefore help the other and Swinton saw clearly the possibilities of a great combined assault which could crush through the enemy line as the British and French had been trying to do since the beginning of 1915. Two requirements were essential. The existence of tanks should be kept secret until a large number were available to go into battle at the same time, thus taking advantage of the surprise that such a weapon, never before seen by the enemy, would undoubtedly cause. And the sector of attack should be chosen carefully on ground most suitable for tanks. Had these two simple and logical suggestions been followed, it is likely that a large-scale assault, spearheaded by tanks, could have broken through the German lines and 'rolled up their front', the objective sought so avidly by Haig when he took over from Sir John French as the British Commander-in-Chief.

Haig appeared at first to agree with Swinton's reasoning. But things on the Western Front in the summer of 1916 were not going well. The Somme offensive on which Haig pinned such hopes had become a disaster, no matter how many unprotected infantry were thrown against the barbed wire and machine guns of the Germans. On July 1st, the opening day of the campaign, the British sustained 60,000 casualties—20,000 of them killed—the heaviest loss ever suffered in a single day by any army during the war. But the generals refused to admit defeat, not of their armies but of their blundering, obstinate ideas, and the slaughter continued. When one night attack almost by accident did achieve a small breakthrough, the moment came to send in the cavalry, the glorious charge with sabres drawn and lances glittering of which the British generals had dreamed for so long. Three divisions of cavalry faltered and fell before a curtain of German machine gun fire. By now, even the public at home was sensing that battles of this kind did not seem to work and criticisms of Haig began to mount.

Haig cast desperately around for some means of sustaining the offensive and decided to throw in the tanks. The crews were insufficiently trained, there were too few tanks available to make a large-scale assault, and the ground, cratered by weeks of shelling, could hardly have been less suitable. Swinton's essential requirements were completely ignored. Both Lloyd George and Winston Churchill, early advocates of the tank, were shocked at such a premature disclosure of the secret weapon. But Haig was adamant. On September 15th 48 tanks, all that were available of the 60 that had been despatched to France by then, joined an attack launched by General Rawlinson's Fourth Army. They were not even massed together but spread thinly along a three mile front between the Combles ravine and Martinpuich. In such a petty and indecisive operation was thrown away the great advantage which the first surprise appearance of tanks might have had.

CHAPTER THREE

Baptism of Fire

The Battle of the Somme had been in progress for nearly ten weeks when the officers and men of the Heavy Section arrived with their tanks at that sector of the front where the Fourth Army, by means of a surprise night attack in mid July, had managed to advance and occupy four miles of devastated country. Most of them had never been to the Western Front before. They found themselves in a strange world in which endless lines of transport crawled over incredibly bad roads bordered by jagged stumps of trees and a tragic litter of dead men and horses and rotting equipment. The Germans were counter attacking over the whole 30 mile front and guns sounded everywhere.

During the nights of September 13th and 14th the tanks, which had been camouflaged, were moved up to the assembly area under a cloak of great secrecy. Driving at night through the mud and in and out of shell holes was extremely difficult, even though white tapes had been laid on the ground for the commanders who were guiding the vehicles by walking in front, and a number broke down or became irretrievably ditched. Of the 48 tanks allocated to the battle, only 32 reached their starting positions in the front line. One tank commander reported that his driver baulked at going down a narrow sunken road strewn with dead bodies.

Equipping the tanks for battle order had been a major problem. Every crew member, the officer and seven men, carried two gas helmets, one pair of goggles, and a leather 'antibruise' helmet in addition to his ordinary service cap and the usual equipment consisting of a revolver, haversack, first aid kit, water bottle and iron rations. All this was dumped on the floor as the crew came aboard. But there was much more. Each tank carried 30 tins of food, 16 loaves, cheese, tea, sugar and milk; drums of engine oil and grease; a spare Vickers machine gun and four replacement barrels, together with 33,000 rounds of ammunition; water-cans, boxes of revolver ammunition, wire cutters, and many other items. A difficult problem still unresolved had been providing a means of communication between tanks in battle and between tanks and the infantry with whom they were operating. A crude wireless transmitter had been designed and fitted into each tank with 100 yards of cable, attached to a second instrument which was to be left at the jumping off place. The cable was to be unwound as the tank advanced and messages relayed to a wireless operator behind. What happened when the tank advanced further was not explained. In any event the device was not used since nothing could be heard anyway above the noise of the engine. Communication between tanks was carried out by displaying metal discs, by semaphore with metal arms, and by morse flag signalling out of the roof manhole. (One officer plaintively recalled that the three flags provided for this purpose were often lost amongst the stores just when they were most needed.) Many tanks carried a more reliable means of communication in the form of two carrier pigeons, the idea being to release them when main objectives were reached so that the battle commander could be informed of progress. The tank commanders were supplied with rice paper on which messages were to be written in code and put into metal tubes attached to the pigeons' legs. (It was not unknown, however, for a tank commander to forget to send these messages in the heat of battle and to choose pigeon pie as one way of destroying the evidence.)

Three days of intensive artillery bombardment preceded the attack, whose objective was to break through the German lines to the important road centre of Bapaume and make way for the cavalry to dash forward and roll up the enemy front northward, as intended in the original plan of July 1st. Ten tanks were to work with the Guards Division and six with the 6th and 56th Divisions on the right, their objectives being Ginchy and the Quadrilateral, while on the left of the front eight tanks were allotted to the III Corps, attacking through High Wood and east of Martinpuich, and eighteen to the XV Corps. The remaining six were attached to the Reserve Army, the 5th Canadian Corps, which was to attack between Pozières and Martinpuich.

The morning of the 15th was fine with a thin ground mist. Although the main attack was not to begin until 6.20am, behind a creeping artillery barrage, the battle was opened one hour earlier by the advance of a solitary tank in a preliminary operation to drive the enemy out of a pocket just ahead of the British front near Delville Wood. This was D 1, under the command of Captain H. W. Mortimore. Two other tanks were also to have been used but one had broken down and the other was ditched. The effect on the Germans, who had never seen such a vehicle before, was electrifying. As the tank crawled towards them out of the mist, shells firing from the bulbous sponsons on either side and a machine-gun spitting from the front turret, many of them fled in terror. The pocket was quickly cleared for the infantry following a quarter of an hour later.

This reaction to the first appearance of tanks was repeated on all parts of the front where they were used, giving some indication of the effect that a massed attack by several hundred tanks would have achieved. The following description was written by a German newspaper correspondent who witnessed the first ever tank attack.

"When the German outposts crept out of their dugouts in the mist of the morning and stretched their necks to look for the English, their blood was chilled in their veins. Mysterious monsters were crawling towards them over the craters. Stunned as if an earthquake had burst around them, they all rubbed their eyes, fascinated by the fabulous creatures

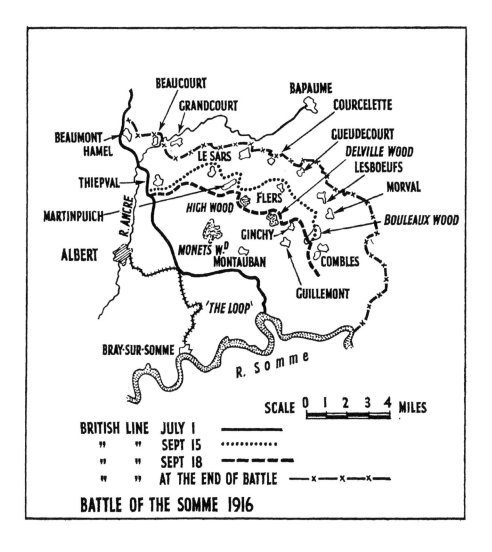

BEAUCOURT
BAPAUME
GRANDCOURT
COURCELETTE
BEAUMONT
HAMEL
GUEUDECOURT
DELVILLE WOOD
LE SARS
LESBOEUFS
THIEPVAL
MORVAL
MARTINPUICH
R. ANCRE
HIGH WOOD
FLERS
BOULEAUX WOOD
ALBERT
MONETS W.D
GINCHY
MONTAUBAN
COMBLES
GUILLEMONT
'THE LOOP'
BRAY-SUR-SOMME
R. Somme

SCALE 0 1 2 3 4 MILES

BRITISH LINE   JULY 1 ——————
    "   "   SEPT 15 ··············
    "   "   SEPT 18 — — — — —
    "   "   AT THE END OF BATTLE —×—×—×—

BATTLE OF THE SOMME 1916

"Their imaginations were still excited by the effects of the artillery bombardment. It was no wonder then that imagination got the better of these sorely tried men, who knew well enough that the enemy would try every means to destroy our steel wall of fragile human bodies. These men no longer knew what fear is. But here was some devilry which the brain of man had invented, with powerful mechanical forces, a mystery which rooted one to the ground because the intelligence could not grasp it, a fate before which one felt helpless.

"One stared and stared as if one had lost the power of one's limbs. The monsters approached slowly, hobbling, rolling and rocking, but they approached. Nothing impeded them; a supernatural force seemed to impel them on. Someone in the trenches said 'the devil is coming', and the word was passed along the line like wildfire.

"Suddenly tongues of flame leapt out of the armoured sides of the iron caterpillars. Shells whistled over our heads and the sound of machine gun fire filled the air. The mysterious creature had yielded its secret as the English infantry rolled up in waves behind the 'devil's coaches'."

One of the men to go into this first tank battle, William Divall, later described the experience in a letter to his sister:

"As the tanks travel over the front trench, the troops rub their eyes in wonder at their strange, cube-impressionist coats of many colours. The deck of the tank rolls and pitches like a torpedo boat in a storm. But we are all old hands—ABs in fact—and we come safely through without seasickness.

"Hun bullets are rebounding from our tough sides like hail from a glass roof. We just crawl over the embankment, guns and all. It is not necessary to fire a single shot. Two or three Huns are brave enough to creep on the back of the tank from behind. We open a small trapdoor and shoot them with a revolver.

"It is almost like playing hide-and-seek as we travel backward and forward along the trench.

"Inside the tank is the crew, strangely garbed, as becomes their strange craft, while around them is a complicated mass of machinery. We succeed in putting out two machine gun emplacements, the guns of which have been worrying our infantry for some time. And now the action begins in earnest. The whole crew are at various guns, which break forth in a devastating fire.

"By this time the fumes from hundreds of rounds which we have fired, with the heat from the engines and the waste petrol and oil, have made the air quite oppressive and uncomfortable to breathe. However, those who go down to the land in tanks are accustomed to many strange sensations, which would make an ordinary mortal shudder.

"We make a fairly difficult target as our way lies between numerous tree trunks and battered stumps, also much barbed wire. We are battling bravely with the waves of earth we encounter. But thanks to our protective headgear, we come through it all.

"The last trench proves to be the worst, for just as we are crossing a large hole, our bus stops. I believe the sparking plugs have ceased to sparkle, and it is a very awkward place as the tree stumps now prevent free traverse of our guns . . .

"And now the old bus is going strong again. Only just in time for a large lyddite bomb bursts against the armoured jacket of my gun. The flare comes in through the port-hole, blinding me for a minute or so, while splinters strike my face. But my gun is still untouched, thanks to the armourplate, and somehow seems to work much better.

"The Germans are now scattered in small parties. After a few short runs we find no more Huns to hunt, so as our objective, the wood, has been gained, we leave the scene to the infantry and find shelter from possible stray shells in a large hole which has been made by many shells.

"After a little exercise we start to overhaul the tanks and guns, in readiness for the next joy ride. Then we snatch a few hours of sleep."

Of the 32 tanks which left their starting positions, nine broke down from mechanical trouble and five became ditched. The remaining 18 met with varying success but the greatest achievement of the day was the assault on the village of Flers, nearly a mile forward. Seven tanks of D Company led the attack by a New Zealand and an English division in the centre of the XV Corps sector. Four were knocked out by direct hits, but by 8.40am three had managed to push on to the outskirts of the village, smashing machine gun posts, breaking down fortified houses, and spreading so much panic among the enemy that most of them fled back along the road to Gueudecourt. D 17 (*Dinnaken*), commanded by Captain Hastie, drove right through the village, followed by parties of infantry who were braced for the usual ordeal of house-to-house fighting, only to find that the enemy had been cleared out by the tanks. They did not suffer a single casualty. It was the furthest penetration achieved by any tank that day and, as it happened, was witnessed by an observer in a British aircraft overhead who sent back a message that was to be widely reported in the British Press: 'A tank is walking up the High Street of Flers with the British Army cheering behind.'

For now the secret was out. The public came to hear about tanks for the first time and the Press had a field day. 'Giant Toad', 'Land Dreadnought', 'Motor Monster' were a few of the descriptions applied to the tanks in wildly exaggerated reports of what they could do, such as smashing down trees like matchwood and leaping over trenches. The German Press on the other hand set up a clamour of protest that tanks were an inhuman and barbarous weapon of warfare to which they had every right to object, as the Allies had done when the Germans first used poison gas. This was quickly changed with the circulation of an official statement that the tank was actually a German invention and that the German General Staff had known all about them for a long time and had already experimented with them. This was of course completely untrue. When the first reports of the new weapon reached the German High Command, there was a moment of panic and a frantic search was made for the Mr Steiner who had approached them with designs for tracked vehicles back in 1912. He could not be found. But when the Germans saw how relatively ineffective the tanks appeared to be, for the simple reason that too few of them were used and in the wrong conditions, they relaxed. And when from experiments with two captured tanks they discovered that the Mark I was vulnerable to ordinary 'K' armour piercing bullets, their initial reaction changed to sneers of contempt that tanks were merely makeshifts to supplement a lack of more orthodox munitions.

This attitude found an echo in British military circles, where much of the scepticism that had previously existed turned to scorn. A few individual tanks had done very well, it was true. In a renewed offensive on September 25th, one female tank in particular was responsible for destroying a German field gun battery, capturing a mile of trench in less than an hour, and taking nearly 400 prisoners at a cost to the attackers of only five casualties, enabling the infantry to seize the village of Gueudecourt with virtually no resistance. But when the tank had to leave because it was running short of petrol, the leading infantry relapsed into over-caution and dug in instead of taking advantage of the breakthrough by pushing on. Late in the afternoon the Germans brought up reinforcements to establish a position one mile north of Gueudecourt and by the time the cavalry squadrons arrived, it was too late to exploit the opportunity.

Only in one minor action in mid-November, as the Somme offensive gradually petered out, did a small group of tanks give an inkling of what they could do if used properly to attack in force. This was on the Fifth Army's sector to the north where, after four months of heavy fighting south of the River Ancre, the Germans had been pushed back beyond Thiepval but still retained a strongly defended salient on high ground around Beaumont-Hamel. The village had been attacked at the start of the campaign but with a complete lack of success. It was now decided to renew the offensive by a surprise attack in the hope of pinching off the salient. All the available tanks had previously been collected, a total of 52, and brought by train to Acheux. Because of bad weather and the soggy state of the ground however, only eight could be brought up to the Front. They arrived by night and preparations were made for the attack to commence early on the morning of November 13th, after a cold spell had begun to dry the ground.

An hour and a half before sunrise, in a thick mist which added to the confusion of the enemy, three tanks of A Company led the attack south of the Ancre by troops of the 39th Division. One soon became stuck in the mud and another broke down with mechanical trouble but the third managed to push on alone across the German trenches and gave considerable help to the infantry as they advanced through St Pierre Divion and gained their final objective shortly after sunrise. The British line was moved forward by one mile. North of the Ancre, five tanks had been made available to the 63rd (Royal Naval) and 51st Divisions, to be used if their attack faltered for any reason. A holdup did occur outside the village of Beaumont-Hamel where the Germans had established a strong network of trenches. Two of the tanks came forward and after several hours of intensive fighting helped to achieve its capitulation. Between the village and the river, the Germans continued to hold out in their front line and support trenches and the remaining three tanks were called up to assist. Two of them arrived at first light on the 14th and lumbered forward across No Man's Land. One succeeded in crossing the German front trench but then became stuck in deep mud. When the second also became stuck before it could even cross the trench, the situation for the crews was highly precarious. They could use their guns of course, but on the other hand the tanks were sitting targets for the German gunners. Such was the awe in which the tanks were held however, that the entire German garrison surrendered on the spot. The scene was described in a letter written by one of the tank officers who was present.

"On examining the ground about them the Officer Commanding the leading tank noticed the whole area appeared to be shimmering with white. On opening the front flap of the tank and obtaining a better view, it was seen that all the German garrison, some 400 in number, appeared to have found something white to wave in token of surrender; those who could not produce anything better were waving lumps of chalk about or bits of board or rifle stocks which they had rapidly chalked white. The situation was rather an embarrassing one for so small a number as the crews of two tanks to deal with; fortunately, however, it was possible by signs and with the assistance of the infantry to 'mop up' these 400 prisoners before they realised that both the tanks were stuck and out of action."

Movement of the tanks over the churned up ground, especially in the hours of darkness, was aided by prior reconnaissance of the battle area by tank commanders and the laying down of white tapes over the planned routes. Most of this work at Beaumont-Hamel, as the fighting continued for another four days, was done by Captain (later Major-General) F. E. Hotblack, then the Intelligence Officer of the Heavy Section and one of the most remarkable of the early tankmen. On one occasion a fall of snow obliterated some of the tapes he had laid. As the only man who knew the terrain, Hotblack led a tank forward on foot to where it was urgently required to deal with an enemy machine gun position. Under a hail of bullets and taking what little advantage he could of ice-filled shell holes he literally walked the tank up to the enemy trench and then returned to report the progress of the action. After the tank had devastated the German position, another urgent call for its services was made from a nearby sector where the infantry advance had also been halted. Since there was no way at that time of signalling this information to the crew, Hotblack again walked across the fireswept ground to guide the tank to a new position. Miraculously he was still not hit. For this daring exploit he was awarded the DSO but a more far reaching result was that it laid the foundations for the subsequent efficiency of the Reconnaissance Branch of the Tank Corps and proved the vital importance of ground intelligence in the planning of future tank operations.

The action at Beaumont-Hamel was broken off on November 18th with most of the German salient captured. At the end of the month the whole Somme offensive finally came to a halt in hopelessly sodden, shell cratered ground. It had been a dismal failure. The Allied front was advanced in a few places by five miles or so, but beyond that the German line was as strong as ever. No breakthrough had been achieved. The British lost some 420,000 casualties and the French nearly 200,000 against a German loss of probably 450,000 and even that would have been less had not the German High Command, with an obstinacy rivalling that of the Allied generals, insisted on retaking trenches by reckless counter attacks. Too few tanks had been available in the first place and they were badly used in twos and threes instead of in one massed attack which might have had a significant effect. Most of them had either been crippled by artillery fire after bogging down in the mud or had to be withdrawn because of mechanical troubles. In the general disillusionment that followed, the tanks were blamed for not fulfilling their earlier promise. Instead of trying to plan for an intelligent use of the superior weapon that had been put in their hands, the military leaders could only make carping criticisms of minor details, conveniently forgetting that it was they who had refused to order larger numbers in the first place and insisted on throwing them into battle before they were mechanically tested or their crews had been properly trained.

The reaction of Haig, who knew better than anyone how the time for preparation and training had been curtailed, was more favourable than that of his staff and subordinate commanders. He admitted to Stern and Swinton, when they visited him at General Headquarters, that: "Wherever the tanks advanced we took our objectives, and where they did not advance we failed to take our objectives." It was at his personal request that 1,000 tanks should be built to an improved design. In order to keep the factories going, a further 100 of the Mark I were built and 50 each of Mark II and Mark III which were similar except they had no tail wheels and thicker armour. But the main effort was concentrated on the new Mark IV for which the design work had just been completed. This was the tank that was to make the first real breakthrough of the war, in the Battle of Cambrai in November 1917, and finally vindicate the efforts of those who believed in tanks. But before that, the tanks were to be subjected to their worst maltreatment of all, in the mud of Flanders.

Top: Officers of the Royal Naval Air Service experimenting with a Killen Strait tractor at Wormwood Scrubbs in June 1915.

Above: Official trials with the Foster-Daimler tractor in 1915 which succeeded in climbing a gradient of 1 in 2½ and then hauled two trucks weighing 16 tons by means of its winding gear.

Top: The Delaunay Belville armoured car, built for the Royal Naval Air Service in 1915.

Above: 'Little Willie' undergoing trials at Lincoln in November 1915, fitted with the Wilson-Tritton track.

Top right: 'Big Willie' was officially designated as His Majesty's Landship *Centipede.*

Centre right: Rear view of HMLS *Centipede*, showing the three doors and the wheels used for steering.

Right: 'Big Willie', or 'Mother' as it was later known, successfully going through its trials at the end of 1915.

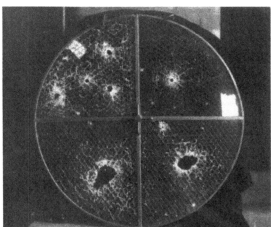

Above: German anti-tank rifle ammunition, compared with British service rifle ammunition (left).

Left: Result of firing test on wired glass, suggested as a material for the portholes of Mark I tanks.

Below left: Firing tests on two polished surfaces, also suggested as a covering for Mark I portholes. Eventually, direct vision through very small peepholes was adopted.

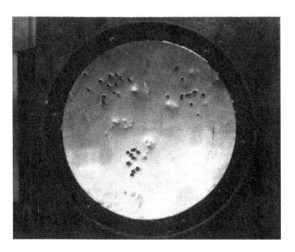

Top: The first official photograph of a tank going into action, at Flers-Courcelette on September 15th, 1916. The crew member is wearing a leather tank helmet and the wire covering is to protect the top surface from grenades thrown by enemy infantry.

Above: German view of one of the first tanks to go into action, partly hidden in mist and the smoke of battle.

Top: A male Mark I armed with 6pdrs, moving up to the front to take part in the Battle of the Somme in September 1916.

Above: Machine gunners wearing gas helmets during the Battle of the Somme.

Right: Vizor of steel and chain mail, provided to protect tankmen from splinters and bullet splash.

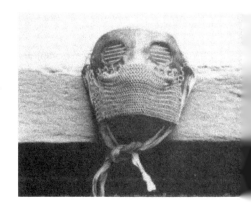

Above: An armoured car helps in the evacuation of wounded on a road near Guillemont in September 1916.

Below: A Mark I of 'C' Company moving towards the front in the area known as Chimpanzee Valley.

Above: One of the first casualties of
shelling, a Mark I with long 6pdr guns.

Below: A section of Mark I tanks,
fuelling for battle.

Above: A Mark I female tank. Note the crew member looking out through the gun sponson and the door beside him which was so small that many became trapped inside their tanks when hit by shell fire.

Below: An armoured car ditched beside the Arras-Tilloy road during the Arras offensive on April 10th, 1917.

Above: Tank and infantry moving up for the Arras offensive.

Below: Armoured cars passing through Arras in April 1917.

Above: Tank and infantry moving up for the Arras offensive.

Below: Armoured cars passing through Arras in April 1917.

Top left: The first French tanks to be used in action were the medium Schneiders, during the April 1917 offensive near Rheims.

Left: The heavy French St Chamond tank was not successful at crossing rough country.

Top: Rear view of the St Chamond, similar in appearance to the original 'Little Willie'.

Above: Machine gunners of the 6th Canadian Brigade, during the successful assault on Vimy Ridge in April 1917.

Top: Battlefield scene during the Battle of Arras in April 1917. An 18pdr battery is in action behind the infantry trenches, with a tank and cavalry horse lines in the background.

Above: British soldiers examine a German gun in a captured gun pit near Arras.

Top: Tanks advancing towards the
Messines Ridge on June 7th, 1917.

Above: Mark IV tanks at the tank park
at Rollencourt.

Top: Portuguese infantry at Locon, June 1917.

Above: Tank park at Rollencourt. The Mark IV in the foreground has its sponson removed, showing the limited amount of space inside.

CHAPTER FOUR

Disaster in Flanders

The first tank operations of 1917 took place during the Arras offensive in April. By this time the new force had become better organised. A new training ground had been established at Bovington Camp near Wool in Dorset (which has remained the home of tanks ever since). Brigadier-General Hugh Elles had been appointed to take command in France of what was still known as the Heavy Section, with headquarters at Bermicourt. He had two brigades of tanks, each comprising two battalions, and a third brigade was being formed to accommodate the arrival of further battalions from Bovington. Each battalion was to comprise 60 tanks, divided into three companies. The original programme had promised 240 of the new Mark IV tanks in time for the spring offensive, but supply difficulties at home and the usual indecisions by the War Office had reduced this number to 96. In the event, none began to arrive until the end of April when the battle was over. The only tanks in France at that time were 60 of the improved Marks I and II which were still vulnerable to armour piercing bullets.

Swinton, the man who had fathered the new force from its inception, had been 'released' from his command in England and returned to his former duties in the War Cabinet Secretariat, ending his connection with tanks until 1934 when he achieved belated recognition by being chosen as Colonel-Commandant of the Royal Tank Corps. But by a lucky chance Swinton's removal was compensated by the appointment of Major J. F. C. Fuller, a former infantry officer, as Elles' chief general staff officer. To begin with he shared the doubts of so many others as to the value of tanks, but once he had seen them at close quarters he quickly became their most ardent advocate. His understanding of tank tactics and strategy was far ahead of his time, later establishing for him a worldwide reputation. An early as February 1917 he wrote what was to become the first manual on tank tactics, defining the tank as a mobile fortress which could escort the infantry into the enemy's defences and emphasizing the necessity for surprise in any attack. This, he considered, meant that the artillery bombardment beforehand should be reduced to a minimum, certainly not more than 48 hours. To the artillery experts at General Headquarters such a suggestion was little short of heresy and the pamphlet was ordered to be withdrawn from circulation. It was the start of a long war that Fuller, a man of genius and imagination, was to wage against the apathy and short-sightedness of GHQ where it was believed that only by massive bombardment could the enemy be softened up and his wire barriers broken down, regardless of the warning this always gave of an impending attack.

In March, while the Allied commanders were enthusiastically planning new offensives on the old pattern, having learned nothing from their failures of the previous two years, the Germans had surprised everyone by quietly withdrawing to the Hindenburg Line, the massive defensive system they had been building during 1916 and early 1917. Chosen for its strategic position rather than to retain a few miles of captured territory this line was four miles deep in places, comprising three distinct trench systems, with 50 yards or more of barbed wire massed in front of each one. Concrete positions were built for machine guns and a network of railways constructed so that troops and supplies could speedily reinforce any particular sector. The Germans considered this 45-mile barrier from Arras to Soissons to be impenetrable. Behind it they planned to stand on the defensive, to enable divisions to be sent to the fighting on other parts of the front and to give them time while their submarines continued the destructive work against British shipping. As they fell back they destroyed everything behind them, including towns, villages and even trees, leaving in their place mines and boobytraps.

While the British Fourth and Fifth Armies laboriously made their way forward through the devastated area to make contact with the enemy, Allenby's Third Army held the sector near Arras where the Hindenburg Line ended. Here was seen to be the chance of making an attack through the old defences to turn the flank of the new line before the Germans could bring up reserves. A surprise attack might have achieved this but in accordance with the stultified thinking at GHQ three weeks of preliminary artillery bombardment was ordered, giving the Germans ample time to bring up reinforcements and to prepare new defensive systems in depth.

The offensive was launched on April 9th. Forty tanks of the 1st Brigade, commanded by Lieutenant-Colonel C. D'A. B. S. Baker-Carr, were divided among the Third Army, 16 each to the VI and VII Corps attacking south of the river Scarpe and eight to the XVII Corps north of the river. A further eight tanks were to co-operate with the Canadian Corps, aimed at capturing Vimy Ridge, while 12 were to work with the Fifth Army on the right wing, near Bullecourt. Once again the Cavalry Corps was massed in the background to exploit any break in the German defences. Except for the area near Bullecourt which was only lightly shelled, the ground over the entire sector had been ploughed up by the artillery bombardment and heavy rain had made it even more unsuitable for tanks.

This was evident on the night of the 8th, even before the attack began. In crossing a valley south of Arras to avoid a long detour, six tanks of C Battalion broke through what was thought to be firm ground and became engulfed in the bog underneath. The scene was described in a letter written by an officer who was present:

"Never shall I forget the scene at Achincourt on the eve of the battle. It was round about midnight when I got there and pitch dark save for the fitful light from the still burning village nearby and the flashes of the guns.

"We had got word of 'trouble near the railway crossing', and trouble indeed there was.

"There, sunk and wallowing in a bog of black mud, were some half dozen tanks—tanks that should by then have been miles ahead and getting into their battle position for the attack at dawn.

"Instead, here were the machines on which so much depended, lying helpless and silent at all sorts of ominous angles, and turned this way and that in their vain struggles to churn their way out of the morass.

"About them were great weals and hummocks of mud and ragged holes brimming with black slime. The crews, sweating and filthy, were staggering about trying to help their machines out by digging away the soil from under their bellies and by thrusting planks and brushwood under their tracks. Now and again an engine would be started up and some half submerged tank would heave its bulk up and out in unsteady floundering fashion, little by little and in wrenching jerks as the engine was raced and the clutch released.

"Then the tracks of a sudden would cease biting and would rattle round ineffectively, the ground would give way afresh on one side, and the tank would slowly heave over and settle down again with a perilous list, the black water awash in her lower sponson. No lights could be shown on account of enemy observation and at any time he might reopen with his heavy artillery which had already been blasting the immediate neighbourhood earlier in the night.

"Altogether it was a desperate and discouraging business for those of us who knew that there were infantry already assembled for the morning's assault, who had practised with us, who looked to us for a lead across the German wire, and who must now do as best they might without us."

With the exception of the eight tanks operating with the Canadians at Vimy, the rest were strung out along the front and tank commanders ordered to act independently against the specific strong points allotted to them. The offensive opened with a great success, with the German front line defence system being captured within an hour. The scene was described as follows by an eye-witness:

"Our bombardment was quite unimaginable—all that could possibly be desired, I should think, for accuracy, evenness and intensity. The final barrage was a really wonderful sight; just at dawn the grey sky ablaze with star shells and coloured rockets all along the line, nothing else to be seen.

"Then when it got a little lighter and the barrage had crept on, we could see thousands of our men popping up from their barely visible 'assembly slits' in the ground and pouring up the slope in a slow moving, loose sort of crowd with no discernible formation, and with and among them, the tanks.

"What with the barrage and the tanks, the defence appears to have just collapsed, and a few minutes and a few casualties gave us possession of a wonderful redoubt that the enemy had lavished extraordinary ingenuity and industry in preparing for many months past."

Four tanks of D Battalion led the way for the infantry to capture the strongly fortified village of Neuville-Vitasse. Eighteen of D and C Battalions helped in the taking of keypoints on Telegraph Hill, although all but four became bogged down in the trenches or were put out of action by direct hits. One tank of C Battalion, *Lusitania* commanded by Second-Lieutenant Weber, achieved a particularly remarkable success in the attack south of the Scarpe. It had been late in starting because of mechanical trouble and the infantry in that sector had become pinned down by machine gun fire. The arrival of the tank completely changed the situation. Its 6pdrs silenced the machine guns and as the tank and the infantry advanced together, the Germans surrendered or retreated in their hundreds. All day the tank cruised up and down the valley, clearing many of the enemy trenches and redoubts and stopping only once to allow the overheated engine to cool. After twelve hours a defective magneto finally brought it to a standstill. It was dark by then, but the Germans were able to keep up a steady fire on the tank by aiming at the pinpoints of light showing through loopholes and chinks in the armour. When it became obvious that the engine would not start, Weber switched off the lights and made preparations to evacuate the vehicle. The problem now was to find out where the British line lay and warn the infantry that the crew would be coming in. Otherwise, in the darkness, they might well be taken for Germans. One of the crew, Sergeant Latham, volunteered to undertake this reconnaissance. He crawled out of the tank and across the ground while bullets from both British and German rifles whined over his head. By a mixture of luck and judgment he succeeded in finding the British lines and warned the garrison not to fire at the rest of the crew who would be following. As it happened a new garrison had just taken over who knew nothing of the derelict tank out in front and they would certainly have taken the crew as enemy raiders. The next day, having obtained a new magneto, Weber and some of his crew set out in the hope of salving the *Lusitania*, only to find the tank had been destroyed by British artillery fire.

Elsewhere on the front, however, the tanks did not fare so well. Because of drenching rain and sleet which started two hours before the attack, the eight allotted to the Canadian Corps all became bogged down in No Man's Land and so played no part in the historic taking of Vimy Ridge. At Bullecourt, which was attacked by the 4th Australian Brigade two days later on the 11th, the situation was far worse. Eleven tanks of D Battalion led the advance, 15 minutes ahead of the Australian infantry. But owing to a misunderstanding, the sound of their approach to the starting line had not been muffled by machine gun fire as intended. Worse still, it had snowed the night before and in the clear light of dawn, the tanks made perfect targets for the German field-guns. Nine were knocked out by direct hits before they even reached the German lines. The remaining two pressed on for about five miles, together with 200 Australians, but all were surrounded and captured because of a failure in advancing the right hand sector of the line. With no tanks to aid them, the Australians lost 2,500 officers and men out of 3,000 by the time they had to withdraw under a fierce German counter attack. This led to much bitterness and distrust among the Australians who felt they had been let down by the tanks, although in reality too much had been expected of them and the plan was insufficiently flexible to take account of the unexpected snowstorm. However, the Australian suspicion of tanks remained until 1918, when their confidence was restored at the Battle of Hamel.

The Arras offensive dragged on until mid May but it was the same old story. After the first success, the Germans brought up fresh reserves and the line became stronger than ever. Before the battles finally petered out in the usual stalemate, small pockets of tanks were again used. But moving over the muddy, churned-up ground was extremely difficult and those that did not break down were still vulnerable to the armour piercing bullet. By the end of the offensive there was hardly an unwounded man amongst the tank crews of the 1st Brigade. Their limited successes had shown what could be done and they dreamed of fighting, just for once, a battle on hard ground suitable for tanks. But before this was to come about, they were to suffer their worst ordeal of all in the Third Battle of Ypres.

Ever since he had become Commander-in-Chief in December 1915, Haig had dreamed of a great offensive in Flanders to break through the Ypres salient where British troops were being slaughtered in attacks from two sides. The biggest problem was the ground itself which was of heavy clay and usually waterlogged because the Belgians had broken the dykes to the north and let in the sea. Artillery bombardment had turned it into a quagmire, deep enough for horses and men to sink out of sight should they stray from the pathways built across the mud. But Haig never visited the front line, in common with most of his senior staff, and he did not intend such impossible conditions to deter him.

The offensive began early in June 1917 with a preliminary success that had little to do with Haig himself. The ridge at Messines, overlooking the salient and in German hands for more than two years, was blown up by one million pounds of explosives, planted in laboriously dug tunnels under the German trenches. The sound of the explosion was so great it could be heard in London. The Tank Corps had at last begun to receive deliveries of the new Mark IV and 40 of these advanced in the first assault. There was little for them to do. The German defences had been shattered and it was a simple task for the British infantry to march in and occupy the ridge. But at the village of Messines, where New Zealand infantry were under heavy fire, it was due to the efforts of a single tank lumbering through the main street that the enemy eventually surrendered.

The new Mark IV tank was a considerable improvement on its predecessors. It was similar in outline to the Mark I but had smaller sponsons that could be far more easily unbolted during transit by rail. The tail wheels had of course already been discarded. The armament was much the same—two

6pdr guns and four machine guns in the male tank and six machine guns in the female—but the armour was improved to give protection for the first time against the German 'K' armour piercing bullets. The risk of fire was decreased by mounting an armoured 60 gallon petrol tank outside at the back of the vehicle instead of carrying two tanks inside the cabin as before. In place of the glass prisms on the Mark I which splintered if hit, sometimes blinding the driver, pinhole perforations were provided in the steel plate which gave a reasonable field of vision. One of the biggest problems during the early battles had been due to ditching, when a tank either became wedged when crossing a trench or bellied on soft ground. The Mark IV had two improvements to overcome this; iron shoes which could be clamped at intervals along the tracks, and a square unditching beam that was carried on top and could be fastened to the tracks, enabling the tank to heave itself out of shellholes or trenches.

Two hundred of these tanks were brought into the Ypres salient to take part in the main assault which was to begin on the last day of July. Three days before that, since there was no longer any need for secrecy, the new force was officially designated The Tank Corps. A distinctive cap and arm badge was issued, depicting a Mark I tank without the rear wheels, and Corps colours of brown, red and green were chosen. The prosaic reason for those particular colours was that they were the only silks available in the draper's shop visited by Elles and one of his brigade commanders to obtain material for the flag. Fuller later aptly suggested that the colours should mean 'from mud, through blood, to the green fields beyond', reflecting the dream of all tankmen at that time of being able to fight on firm ground in open country. But for the moment, it had to remain a dream. In Flanders, it was only mud and blood for the new Corps.

The offensive commenced with a heavy artillery bombardment which lasted for thirteen days. Over four million shells were fired from 3,000 guns—one gun to every six yards of the 11 mile frontage of attack. The ground was churned into a terrible state which became even worse when it began to rain on the night before July 31st, rain that was to continue non-stop for several weeks. The conditions could not have been more unsuitable for tanks, for which the Somme experience was merely a prelude. General Elles expressed increasing misgivings, only to be told that "guns were the big thing, and tanks must take their chances".

General Gough's Fifth Army had been brought up to make the main attack with nine divisions, supported by another ten. The first day's objective was to advance two miles to the German third line. Then the artillery would be moved forward to provide support for the next assault on Passchendaele ridge, two miles farther on. After that had been taken the next advance would take the Fifth Army to Roulers, 12 miles from Ypres, and then the way would be open for the cavalry to exploit the breach and a great breakthrough might be made to Ostend and Zeebrugge. Haig was planning a decisive victory that would force the Germans to sue for peace before the Americans joined the war. But it was doomed from the start, as the knowledge of what had transpired in previous battles might well have shown.

The 216 fighting tanks were divided into three groups, one to clear strongpoints on the enemy's second line, one to aid the infantry's advance to the third line, and one to be held in reserve. The attack began at 3.50am in a blanket of mist and drizzling rain. Although the German front line fell almost immediately, the tanks were in trouble for the very start as they slithered through the mud and shell craters. Many of the 136 tanks which moved forward as dawn broke became stuck before they had gone more than a few yards, sitting targets for the German guns and low flying aircraft. The tanks of the 2nd Brigade suffered the worst as they tried to help the II Corps take Gheluvelt Plateau. Their only route was along narrow defiles between three heavily guarded woods. Only four of the first 16 succeeded in running the gauntlet of enemy artillery fire to catch up with the infantry and even these were later knocked out. Fourteen of the next echelon of 24 got through but could make little progress in the mud. Reserve tanks were called up but only one made it through the woods. It was hardly surprising that the area became known as the tank graveyard.

By midday, although over half the tanks were out of action, the situation looked promising. The infantry had advanced to their objectives on all sectors of the front, except that of II Corps, and captured some 6,000 prisoners. But the position was deceiving. The Germans had intentionally thinned out their forward lines, keeping the main strength of their Fourth Army to the rear. The 13 days of bombardment had given them all the advance warning they needed of the attack. In the afternoon they launched a heavy counter attack against the six British divisions which were advancing towards Passchendaele Ridge. The British were pushed back to their first objective on the line of the Steenbeek. At the end of the day the leading divisions had been reduced to half their fighting strength while only 19 of the tanks that had moved forward in the morning were still operational. The battleground was strewn with derelict wrecks, some nearly submerged in mud, others burnt out or with their tracks shot away.

Heavy rain during the next four days prevented further fighting and reduced the shelled areas at the front to a quagmire over two miles wide. Haig's own despatch reported: "The low lying clayey soil, torn by shells and sodden with rain, turned into a succession of vast muddy pools. The valleys of the choked and overflowing streams were speedily transformed into long stretches of bog, impassable except by a few well defined tracks, which became marks for the enemy's artillery. To leave these tracks was to risk death by drowning, and in the course of the subsequent fighting on several occasions both men and pack animals were lost in this way."

Behind the bald words of that report lay the indescribable misery of the Third Battle of Ypres. It was one thing to write of such conditions but quite another matter to experience them—and Haig never did visit the front himself. When his Chief of Staff did so, after the battle, he broke down and cried tearfully, "Good God, did we really send men to fight in that?"

Although the weather and the strength of the German counter attack had dashed all hopes of the great breakthrough, Haig still persisted, pinning his faith now on a policy of attrition for the sole purpose of killing Germans, no matter how many casualties the British also suffered. The assault was renewed on August 10th and so began the long and futile mudbath battle which, in the words of the British Official History, 'discouraged all ranks more than any other operation fought by British troops in the war.' Day after day the infantry struggled waist deep in mud for the gain of a few yards of ground, only to lose it again in German counter attacks. The few remaining tanks were thrown in to what was now their inevitable fate of bogging down and becoming helpless targets for German guns. Sometimes they were able to put up a fight, due to the sheer courage and perseverance of their exhausted crews. One such occasion was on the morning of October 4th during an attack north of Gheluvelt by the 21st Division, assisted by a section of tanks from A Battalion. For three days and nights previously the section commander, Captain Clement Robertson, and his batman, Private Allen, had reconnoitred backwards and forwards over the ground, always under fire, to tape routes for the tanks. But on the morning of the attack it was too dark and misty for the tank commanders to see the tapes. Since he knew the ground so well by now, Captain Robertson walked ahead to guide them across a bridge to their positions, emulating Hotblack's similar action at the Somme a year earlier. The enemy fire became increasingly intensive but it was not until he had succeeded in leading the tanks to their objective that Robertson was shot and killed. He was awarded the first Victoria Cross to be won by the Tank Corps. (Private Allen was subsequently given the DCM.)

It was not until November 6th, after a final attack which resulted in the capture of the ruined village of Passchendaele, that the offensive was called off. Three months of bloody fighting had cost the British over 300,000 casualties as against under 200,000 German. But for what? The total ground gained was no more than four miles and the British line was left in a more awkward salient than before. The morale, not only of the tank crews but of the British Army as a whole, reached its lowest ebb. Even the generals were beginning to realise that something was wrong, that battles in the old style did not seem to work, no matter how many men were sent into the mincing machine. Except for Haig perhaps, who went on blithely preparing for a renewal of the campaign in the following spring. It was of Haig and Kiggell, his Chief of Staff, that Fuller wrote after the war:

"They considered that their doctrine of war was infallible, that the wearing battle must succeed if sufficient reinforcements were forthcoming and that as ultimately this doctrine demands an onslaught of cavalrymen, without cavalry the battle could not be won. The truth I believe is that long before the outbreak of war their brains had become ossified and that even the terrible circumstances of this battle would not penetrate the historic concrete in which they were encased. If this is not the true explanation, then Haig and Kiggell must have been two of the greatest knaves in the history of war, which I cannot believe."

The extraordinary reluctance to accept that new technologies, as typified by the tank, were changing the whole concept of warfare was evidenced by one Army Commander who stated after the Ypres campaign: "One, tanks are unable to negotiate bad ground; two, the ground on a battlefield will always be bad; therefore, three, tanks are no good on a battlefield." This was certainly true as regards the battles in which they had been used, or rather misused. It led to further doubts at the War Office in London about the value of tanks and for a while the fate of the new Corps hung in the balance. But although few realised it at the time, Passchendaele was the last of the senseless battles of attrition, fought in the hopelessness and despair of being able to conceive any other way of waging war. For on another part of the front the Tank Corps had quietly been planning an attack in conditions of their own choosing, on dry hard ground, instead of being thrown away in situations in which they were virtually useless. The location chosen was near the town of Cambrai, 45 miles south of Ypres. It was there that the first real tank battle in history was fought and tanks proved for the first time what they could achieve if used properly. The Battle of Cambrai was to revolutionise modern warfare and pave the way for final victory the following year.

CHAPTER FIVE

Breakthrough at Cambrai

Cambrai lay seven miles behind the Hindenburg Line, a sector of the front commanded by General Sir Julian Byng's Third Army. It was a region of open, rolling countryside and firm ground covered by uncultivated grass that had seen little fighting during the war. The Germans considered their fortifications to be impregnable and were content to remain behind them on the defensive while the Allies wore themselves out in reckless assaults elsewhere. During August, while the fighting in Flanders continued its senseless course, Fuller, now promoted to Lieutenant-Colonel, had suggested this as an ideal place in which to mount a tank attack. What he had in mind was a major raid, not for the purpose of taking ground but to destroy or capture enemy troops and guns.

The idea was at first given a very lukewarm reception at Haig's General Headquarters, housed within the dark walls of the old Vauban fortress at Montreuil. Everyone was too busy with the Flanders campaign to have time to consider an attack anywhere else, and some staff officers could not resist pointing out, quite unfairly, that the tanks were not doing well at Ypres. Why should they do better at Cambrai? The reason was obvious to Fuller and the Tank Corps but not to their hidebound military leaders. However, support for the plan came from another direction. General Byng had already been thinking of making an attack with his Third Army in the Cambrai area and the possibility of using tanks appealed to him. Rather too much so, in fact, for what had originally been conceived as a quick in-and-out raid was gradually built up into a major assault for the purpose of gaining ground. Fuller had serious doubts about the wisdom of this but no one liked to dampen Byng's enthusiasm, especially as the Tank Corps had none too many supporters at that time.

As the initial preparations went ahead, further support for a major assault came, ironically, from Haig himself. As the weeks dragged on it was becoming clear even to the most obstinate that the Flanders offensive was a failure. Against a rising tide of casualties, faith in the generals was waning fast. Haig wanted to mount a quick operation that had a good chance of showing immediate results in order to raise morale both at home and among his own troops. He was more aware than most of how the tanks had been misused both on the Somme and at Ypres, since he had been largely responsible, and he seized on the Tank Corps plan to achieve some spectacular result in the hope of allaying the criticism being mounted against him. If it failed, he could always blame the tanks as not being capable of fulfilling their earlier promise. In such an event it was not likely that the Tank Corps could have survived. In mid October he gave his approval for the Cambrai attack to take place on November 20th.

The conditions for it were not nearly as favourable by then. The battles in Flanders had drained the Army's resources, most divisions were battle weary and under strength, and on top of all that the collapse of the Italian front at Caporetto on October 24th meant rushing five British divisions to Italy to hold the line, leaving the British Army short of reserves. Nevertheless, plans for the Cambrai attack became even more ambitious. It now took on the form of a full scale battle.

Byng's intention, briefly, was to break through the German defence system along a six mile front between two canals, the Canal de L'Escaut on the right and the Canal du Nord on the left. This was to be accomplished by three brigades of Mark IV tanks, followed by six infantry divisions with support from another two and three more held in reserve. While the tanks and infantry captured the two main features of the area, the ridges of Flesquières and Bourlon, five cavalry divisions (including the Canadian Cavalry Brigade) were to pour through the gap and isolate the town of Cambrai. The German forces would be cut off and rounded up, then the way would be clear to drive northeast towards Valenciennes. From then onwards the plan was rather vague—perhaps in their hearts none of the commanders really believed in its success after all the previous failures to make a breakthrough—but it held to Haig's ultimate doctrine of attacking the German flanks and 'rolling up the front.' (This never did happen, even during the final battles of 1918.) Supporting the attack would be 1,000 guns of the Royal Artillery and 14 squadrons of the Royal Flying Corps which had been recently formed. This co-operation for the first time between tanks and aircraft laid the groundwork for later military tactics which culminated in the decisive German *blitzkriegs* of World War II.

Cambrai, on the river Scheldt, was itself an important target. It had been in German hands since August 1914 and was a major centre of communications where four railways and a number of main roads and waterways converged. One of the railway lines which ran laterally along the German front was a major supply source of men and materials to the various sectors. The German defences in this region were therefore particularly strong. They lay in a wide path, up to $5\frac{1}{2}$ miles deep, between the British front and Cambrai, constructed to take the best advantage of the ridges and spurs that marked the terrain. The three main lines of trenches were dug much wider than usual, up to 16ft, and to a depth of 18ft. Even if tanks were used, and the Germans did not take them very seriously at this time, they were confident that such vehicles would not be able to cross. Each trench system included concrete dugouts in which were massed batteries of machine guns and lay behind acres of dense barbed wire, nowhere less than 50 yards thick. British observers had estimated it would take five weeks of artillery bombardment to cut down this wire in the normal way, at a cost of some £20million in ammunition.

Fuller had given a great deal of thought to the best method of attack by the tanks. He reckoned they could crush through the barbed wire, although there was always a danger of its becoming entangled in their tracks. But the sheer size of the trenches was the biggest problem. An answer was provided by the Central Workshops of the Tank Corps. Bundles of brushwood of the kind used for road repairs were bound together by thick chains to make huge fascines, each weighing nearly two tons. One would be carried on the roof of each tank, to be dropped into the trenches to form a bridge across. The workshops had to work day and night for three weeks to make the 376 fascines required. Some 21,000 bundles of brushwood had to be collected, as well as 2,000 fathoms of heavy steel chain, sources of supply including ship-yards and railings from parks throughout Britain.

The tactics eventually devised by Fuller were based on an ingenious system of leapfrogging for which the tanks were formed into sections of three, operating together. The advance tank was to go forward through the German wire, flattening it for the oncoming infantry. When it came to the first trench it would not cross but turn left and drive parallel along the edge, shooting down the enemy to protect the two main body tanks following behind. One of these was to drop its fascine in the trenches at a selected spot, cross over and also turn left to attack along the other side of the trench. The third tank meanwhile would also cross over and make for the next line of trenches where it would drop its fascine and engage the enemy there. Meanwhile the advance tank would return from its operations on the first trench system, cross over the two trenches and make for the third where it would finally cast the fascine it had been carrying all along. The way would then be open for the tanks to advance into open country beyond the trenches. Three platoons of infantry were to follow closely behind each tank section to capture and garrison the trenches as they were overcome. Finally, special wire-pulling tanks would roll up the flattened wire to make broad pathways for the cavalry advance. In addition to these and the 376 fighting tanks, others were specially equipped for carrying supplies and guns, making a grand total of 474, the largest number that had ever been gathered in one place.

Fuller's plan was approved by Third Army HQ, although he was concerned that none of the fighting tanks were allocated to reserve. Of more importance was the refusal of one commander, Major-General G. M. Harper of the 51st Highland Division, to co-operate. He had been one of those who had opposed the development of machine-guns. Now he thought that tanks were 'unmilitary'. When told he had to employ them, along with the other divisions, he insisted that his tanks should turn right instead of left after crossing the trenches. This was childish obstinacy for although it did not matter which way the tanks turned, it was naturally preferable that they all went the same way. He also divided his tanks into sections of four instead of three, told them to move in line abreast instead of in Vee formation, and kept his infantry at least 100 yards behind them. It was of course vital for tanks and infantry to work closely together. The tanks could deal with

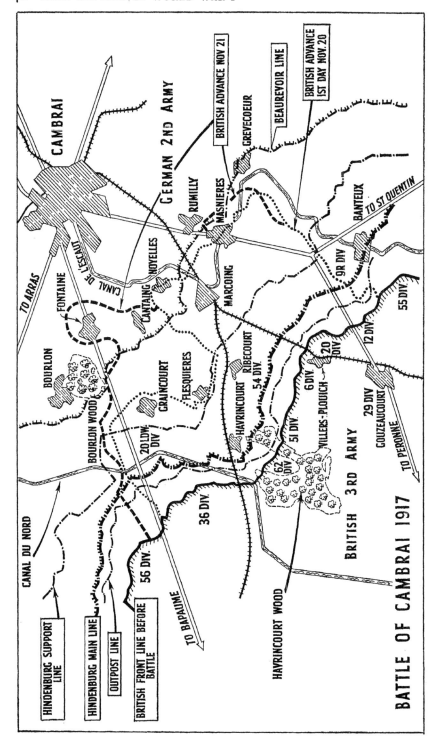

BATTLE OF CAMBRAI 1917

machine gun positions which would have massacred the infantry, but on the other hand needed the infantry to deal with field guns which were little problem to the infantry but from which the tanks were highly vulnerable. Harper's obstinacy led to tragic consequences when the battle started and led to the only major holdup during the first attack which had a profound effect on the entire operation. The Tank Corps complained to the Third Army staff but the doctrine of delegation of command was so deep rooted and the idea of criticising a commander was such an anathema that Harper was allowed to go his own way.

During the week before the attack was due to begin, the tanks were brought up to the front in great secrecy, arriving by night so that even the British infantry did not know of their presence. As darkness fell late in the afternoon of November 19th, the tanks began to leave their hidden lying-up positions in woods and under camouflage in fields and made for their starting places on the front line. One of the section commanders, Captain D. E. Hickey of H Battalion, described the approach march of his three tanks:

"At about five o'clock we left Dessart Wood on our approach march to Beaucamp. A white tape, about two inches wide with a black line along the centre, had been laid over the whole distance. The officer walked in front of his tank to be able to see the tape and direct the driver, guiding him by the glow of a cigarette. A tank was not allowed to go astride the tape for fear of ripping it up.

"About midnight we reached our jumping-off place, taking up a position behind a hedge. The four miles of approach march had taken seven hours—an average speed of little more than half a mile an hour. The rollers of the tanks were greased up and the men turned in to snatch a few hours sleep inside the tanks."

Dawn came up very slowly, grey and overcast with a fine ground mist. The shapes of the woods and ridges ahead began to emerge out of the darkness. The rolling expanse of matted grass was a kind of greyish green, broken by brown patches of withered thistles. Coveys of partridges sprang up and larks and crows took to the sky as the British infantry began to cut through their own wires, ready for the assault. There was no sign of the Germans, hidden deep in their trenches and dugouts. Only the long lines of dense barbed wire.

At zero hour, 6.20am, there was a devastating blast as one thousand British guns opened up a creeping barrage.

"Suddenly, the air itself seemed to reel under a tremendous blow. A dull and curiously mellow roar broke forth and continued with a peculiar rhythm. The atmosphere became alive with the scream of shells. On the opposite slope we could see them bursting on the German trenches while behind these there was a huge black curtain, thrown up by our smoke shells. As they landed they gave the effect of the embers of a burning haystack. Splinters of flame were on every side like exploding stars in the night sky. The Germans were sending SOS rockets from their trenches all along the line. They shone out vividly against the black curtain beyond."

That was how one tank commander described the opening of the artillery bombardment. But instead of continuing for days and even weeks, giving the Germans ample warning of a coming attack and time to bring up reinforcements, almost immediately the barrage began to lift towards targets further ahead while the tanks lumbered forward. At last they were to be used in a surprise attack as the pioneers of their development had always intended. This time it was their responsibility to cut through the barbed wire and make paths for the following infantry.

"It seemed almost too good to be true," reported a tank crew member later, "this steady rumbling forward over marvellous going, no craters in the ground, no shelling from the enemy, and our infantry following steadily behind. Emerging out of the gloom, a dark mass came steadily towards us—the German wire. It appeared absolutely impenetrable. It was certainly the thickest and deepest I had ever seen, stretching in front of us in three belts, each about 50 yards deep. It neither stopped our tank nor broke up and wound round the tracks as we had feared, but squashed flat as we moved forward and remained flat. A broad carpet of wire was left behind us, as wide as our tank, over which the infantry were able to pick their way without any difficulty."

In one of the leading tanks was General Elles, carrying the Corps flag and insisting on the right to lead his men into the first major tank battle in history. It was one of the few occasions in World War I that a general did so and was the spiritual awaking of the Tank Corps, becoming as legendary as his message to the tank crews which was read out by every tank commander the night before.

Special Order No 6

1. Tomorrow the Tank Corps will have the chance for which it has been waiting for many months—to operate on good going in the van of the battle.
2. All that hard work and ingenuity can achieve has been done in the way of preparation.
3. It remains for unit commanders and tank crews to complete the work by judgement and pluck in the battle itself.
4. In the light of past experience I leave the good name of the Corps with great confidence in their hands.
5. I propose leading the attack in the centre division.

Hugh Elles, Brig-Gen
Commanding Tank Corps

The sight of so many tanks lumbering forward in the half light of dawn, their huge fascines on top making them appear even more like monstrous, prehistoric animals, was too much for many of the Germans, who fled in panic. Those who remained were dismayed to find that the armour piercing bullets

Top: Mark IV tanks in action during the Flanders campaign. The one on the left has been hit by enemy artillery and is on fire.

Above: Mark IVs under construction at the Foster factory in Lincoln.

Top left/Left/Above: The Ypres
battlefield was a graveyard for many
tanks which did not have a chance
after becoming stuck in the mud.

Below: Tanks plough their way through
a wood en route for Ypres.

Top left: And this was what they found when they reached the battlefield, the remains of what was once another wood, completely destroyed by shelling. Tank officers confer during the attack on Zonnebeke, September 20th, 1917.

Left: A derelict Mark I of 'D' Company and the graves of its crew near Courcelette, September 21st, 1917.

Above: The Ypres battlefield was strewn with wrecks like these.

Above: A model of the tank attack at Cambrai on November 20th, 1917, showing tanks crossing the Hindenburg Line.

Left: An Australian Lewis gun team in a front line trench at Garter Point, near Ypres.

Above: A tank going through barbed wire during training at Wailly.

Below: In October 1917, all the available Mark IV tanks were gathered at special staging posts in preparation for the great tank attack at Cambrai. Here at Wailly is a tank of 'F' Company with its mascot and officers of the Tank Corps.

This is the view that the terrified German troops had of tanks as they loomed over the parapets of their trenches at Cambrai.

Top: Men of the 11th Leicester
Regiment (6th Division) in a captured
second line trench at Ribecourt, a few
hours after tanks broke through the
Hindenburg Line on the morning of

November 20th.

Above: Another captured trench near
Havrincourt, taken over by the 11th
Inniskilling Fusiliers.

Top: A 'C' Battalion tank drags a captured 5.9in naval gun from a wood east of Ribecourt.

Above: A section of the Hindenburg Line and its barbed wire defences, captured in the Battle of Cambrai.

Top: One tank which did not make it—
Hyacinth of 'H' Battalion, ditched in a
captured German trench.

Above: A Mark IV tank at Cambrai.
The 6pdr guns could swivel round in an
arc of 100 degrees.

Two views of a Mark IV tank presented by the British government to the President of the Federal Council of the Malay States.

Top: Tanks being brought by rail to the railhead at Fins after the Cambrai battle.

Above: This Mark IV was captured by the Germans at the Battle of Cambrai and used during their great offensive in March 1918.

Top right: The Medium Mark A or Whippet, the new British light tank built for the campaigns of 1918.

Centre right: Germans towing away another captured British tank during their March offensive.

Right: A captured British Mark IV being used by the Germans as they advance towards Amiens.

Top: The new and the old way of waging war; French armoured cars and dead horses on a road at St Venant, April 1918.

Above: A tank crew take time off to cook a meal during a lull in the German offensive.

of their machine guns would not penetrate these new tanks. And when the tanks opened up their own fire with 6pdrs and blazing machine guns, the demoralisation of the enemy was complete.

Not that it was a joyride to be inside one of the tanks. The heat was suffocating, the noise ear-piercing, and many among the crews collapsed into unconsciousness. Mr F. R. J. Jefford, MBE, was one of the tank commanders and recalls his experiences of that day:

"I finished up with only the driver and myself conscious, due to the escape of exhaust gas in the pipe from the engine. The crew were so badly affected that they were sent straight back to England. The driver and I escaped the gas, having the advantage of fresh air coming through the front flaps. At one stage of the battle I was faced with the rest of my crew unconscious, the engine stopped, and the enemy firing on my tank. It required four men to work the starting handle, so I had to shake three of the crew alive to get the engine started so we could drive back to safety.

"It took all one's wits to watch the course of the battle from the enclosed world inside the tank. Firstly, we used the periscope to judge the effect of our firing. Secondly, by lifting the shutters of the peep holes, we could watch the fate of other tanks next to us, which wasn't pleasant when they were hit. It was also important to watch the visual compass in order to know one's direction if it became necessary to get out of difficulties quickly. It was extremely difficult to concentrate the gunners on the required target when under shell or machine gun fire. The gunners on the 6pdrs had vertical gaps through which to aim their telescopic sights but inside the tank, when machine guns sprayed our armoured plating, it was like the sparks flying around in a blacksmith's forge. When I was using my forward machine gun, it was impossible to sustain firing for any length of time, as the hot sparks hit my hand and wrist. My skin was mottled for days afterwards."

By midday the tanks had broken through the three trench systems of the Hindenburg Line for the first time in the war and advanced nearly five miles on a 13,000 yard front, a deeper penetration than that achieved after three months fighting at Passchendaele. Over 100 guns and 8,000 prisoners were taken, apart from thousands more killed and wounded, as against only 4,000 British casualties. So great was the contrast with Passchendaele in fact that when the news was received in London, church bells were rung for the first time since the war had started to acclaim a great victory. Meanwhile, at the headquarters of the German Supreme Command, there was consternation and near panic. General Erich Ludendorff, commanding the German armies, ordered an immediate counter attack but as news came through showing the extent of the British advance, this possibility became increasingly remote. Reinforcements were ordered up but they could not arrive for at least 48 hours. In every previous Allied attack, the preliminary bombardment had always given the Germans ample time to make plans and have reserve troops ready. Now the value of a quick surprise attack became evident. So seriously was the situation taken that Ludendorff was forced to consider an extensive withdrawal of the whole Cambrai front, one which might well have led to a general retreat.

But the success of the attack had also taken the British General Staff by surprise. In fact, many of the commanders simply could not believe it. Valuable time was lost while they awaited confirmation of the reports being despatched from the front. The objectives of that morning, with one important exception, had been taken with such relative ease that there was a tendency for the advancing infantry unit to rest on their laurels in the German trenches they had captured, far more comfortable than the British ones they had left behind. In a number of instances they failed to keep up with the tanks which had spearheaded the attack and which later had to withdraw because of lack of support. But there still remained the cavalry, five divisions of which were massed behind the British lines waiting for a breakthrough. They had been waiting for such a chance in nearly every battle that had previously been fought. And now the great breakthrough had been made. They came trotting up to the front in all their glory, described by Mr Keyworth who was serving in a tank of the 9th Battalion.

"On our way towards Cambrai, we were overtaken by the finest body of men I had ever seen. They were the Bengal Lancers. Every man was over six feet tall and they were mounted on beautiful horses. They had wonderful clothing with a large sash round the waist. Their tunics were the best I had ever seen. They were equipped with a carbine, a sword, and in the right hand carried a long lance. Every man's head was covered with a turban."

The way should have been clear for the 1st Cavalry Division to pass through the village of Flesquières in the centre of the attack and move on to assist in taking the all important objective of Bourlon Wood which was on the ridge covering the approach to Cambrai. But it was at Flesquières that the one holdup of the morning had occurred. The attack in that sector had been made by General Harper's 51st Highland Division. The Highlanders had a well earned reputation for tough, determined fighting—their division was one of the most feared by the Germans. Harper himself was widely respected as a fearless leader, intensely proud of his division. But he was a soldier of the old school who had no time for new gadgets like tanks. He ignored the tactics recommended by the Tank Corps and his attitude was echoed by his junior commanders. From the very start of the battle there was a marked absence of co-operation between the infantry and the tank crews. This led to tragic results on Flesquières Ridge.

Harper's men had advanced with the main attack and achieved the apparently impossible by capturing the Hindenburg Main Line by 8.30am. The German front line forces were in full retreat and on other sectors of the front the British commanders took full advantage of the situation by pressing on with the attack ahead of the scheduled timetable. But Harper obstinately decided to stick rigidly to the set plan, which gave his men and the tank crews a rest for an hour but also gave the Germans a chance to gather their scattered forces on the other side of Flesquières Ridge. Even this would not necessarily have been disastrous, but when Harper renewed the attack at 9.30, he continued with his earlier tactics of keeping the infantry well behind the tanks, in spite of the fact that the tanks alone had been responsible for the earlier breakthrough.

Up the slope of the ridge rumbled the tanks of D and E battalions, cutting paths through the barbed wire for the infantry who were at least 400 yards behind. By the time the infantry reached the wire, they had to waste valuable minutes in looking for these paths. Then, suddenly, machine gun fire opened up from Flesquières village to the right where the Germans had managed to take up a defensive position because of Harper's delay in advancing. Had the tanks and infantry been together, the tanks could easily have dealt with the machine guns. As it was, the infantry were unprotected and after suffering heavy casualties, they had to fall back.

Meanwhile, the tanks were pressing on alone towards the crest of the ridge. Unknown to the crews, the Germans on the other side had managed to drag out four 77mm gun batteries and now had them aimed at the top of the ridge. As the tanks appeared, they opened fire. Now it was the turn of the tanks to be unprotected. Had the infantry been with them, they could have dealt with the gun crews in a matter of minutes. But without such support, the tanks were helpless. They made perfect targets for the guns. As the crews worked des-perately at the cumbersome gears to turn the tanks round, the gunners inside found it impossible to take accurate aim with all the pitching and tossing that such a maneouvre entailed. One by one the tanks were hit, until sixteen had been destroyed. Most were on fire and those crew members who had not been killed outright by the bursting shells were burned to death. There were no survivors.

The German gun batteries were destroyed shortly after this by other tanks which had outflanked them, but by now a fierce battle was taking place in Flesquières village which the Germans were valiantly defending. The British divisions on either side had advanced to their objectives and with the Germans in full retreat on these sectors towards Cambrai, the way was clear for Bourlon Ridge to be occupied. Even the cavalry had been able to advance in some areas but the main body which was to pass through Flesquières was inevitably held up. They could of course have gone round the village but it was here that yet another example of poor leadership became apparent. The local cavalry commanders were prevented by the strict doctrine of command from taking the initiative. They could not deviate from the set plan except by direct order from Cavalry Corps HQ—which, as was usually the case, had been established miles behind the British front line. The cavalry had to wait while information on the battle's progress was transmitted back to headquarters and new orders sent forward. By then it was too late to take advantage of the fleeting oppor-tunities that had been offered. The fight for Flesquières continued throughout the afternoon and also held up the advance of the 62nd and 6th Divisions on either side who were nervous of exposing their flanks. When Major-General Braithwaite, commanding the 62nd Division, offered to help by attacking

Flesquières from the rear, Harper refused, apparently feeling that this would be some kind of stigma on his 51st Division. Following the orthodox doctrine which insisted on a uniform advance, Braithwaite ordered his own division to halt and so lost the chance of taking Bourlon without a fight. The opportunity was not to occur again.

By the end of the day, the British had achieved a remarkable success—but it could have been even more decisive. The holdup at Flesquières, which was evacuated by the Germans during the night, had serious consequences. Although the advance continued the following day, its impetus was beginning to run down. Of the 376 tanks which had moved forward at the start of the battle, 179 were out of action. Many of those remaining had been fighting almost continually for sixteen hours and required maintenance services. On the German side, fresh reserves were arriving to strengthen the defences around Cambrai. Haig did in fact see the danger. But having provided the British public at home with a victory, and done something to revive his sagging reputation after the failure in Flanders, he did not wish to call a halt. The offensive continued.

Bourlon Ridge, overlooking the road to Cambrai, now became the main objective. At the crown of the ridge was Bourlon Wood, some 600 acres of thick woodland which gave a great advantage to the defence, while on the lower slope on the far side was Bourlon village. After preparations had been made on November 22nd, including the transportation forward of field artillery and bringing up fresh infantry battalions together with those tanks which were still available for battle, the attack was resumed on November 23rd. But that one day had also given the Germans time to reinforce their positions. They discarded the possibility of a general withdrawal.

The British attack that day was very nearly successful. Most of the wood was taken and, with the help of tanks, the infantry managed to fight their way into Bourlon village. Meanwhile another body of B and C Battalion tanks skirted the wood and forced their way through to the village of Fontaine which was only two miles from Cambrai. In fact a section of tanks had reached this village at the start of the battle, the high point of the British advance on the first day, but had been compelled to withdraw because of the holdup at Flesquières. On that occasion there had been little resistance but now the Germans had had a chance to reorganise their defences. After a day of fierce fighting, the tanks were again forced to withdraw. For another four days the battle swung first one way, then another. At one time the British infantry succeeded in capturing the whole of Bourlon village, only to be driven out a few hours later by a determined German counter attack. The fighting reached its peak in Fontaine on November 27th, described by Philip Gibbs who was then a war correspondent for the *Daily Telegraph*.

"I think no man may look into it now and live after his view—neither an English soldier nor a German one—because the little narrow streets which go between its burnt and broken houses are swept by bullets from our machine guns in the south and the enemy's in the north, and no human being could

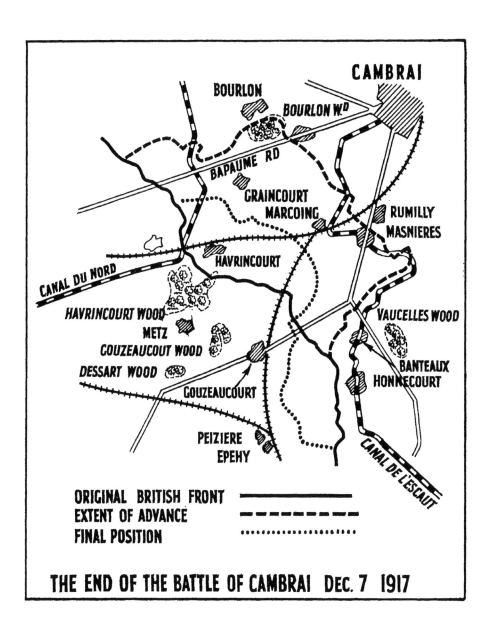

CAMBRAI

BOURLON
BOURLON W.^D
BAPAUME RD
GRAINCOURT
MARCOING
RUMILLY
MASNIERES
HAVRINCOURT
CANAL DU NORD
HAVRINCOURT WOOD
METZ
GOUZEAUCOUT WOOD
DESSART WOOD
GOUZEAUCOURT
VAUCELLES WOOD
BANTEAUX
HONNECOURT
PEIZIERE
EPEHY
CANAL DE L'ESCAUT

ORIGINAL BRITISH FRONT ————
EXTENT OF ADVANCE – – – –
FINAL POSITION ·················

THE END OF THE BATTLE OF CAMBRAI DEC. 7 1917

stay alive there for a second after showing himself in the village . . . Men fought in the streets and in the broken houses and behind the walls and round the ruins of the little church of Notre Dame."

The village became an inferno of shell and machine gun fire, grenades and the cold steel of bayonets. It was the kind of fighting rare during World War I and for which the tanks had no previously prepared tactics.

"There was horrible slaughter in Fontaine," Fuller wrote afterwards, "and I, who had spent three weeks before the battle in thinking out its probabilities had never tackled the subject of village fighting. I could have kicked myself again and again for this lack of foresight, but it never occurred to me that our infantry commanders would thrust tanks into such places."

At the end of the day, the Germans were still holding out at the northern end of the village. The situation at Bourlon was much the same, with the village and part of the wood still in German hands. Haig had no other alternative but to call off the offensive. There were just not enough reserves to keep it going. One week of fighting had achieved little more than the success gained during the first few hours of the battle but on the credit side, apart from the ground that had been captured, over 10,500 German prisoners had been taken, together with 142 guns, 350 machine-guns, 70 trench mortars and large quantities of ammunitions and stores. After a hurried conference at General Headquarters, it was decided to withdraw to a defensive line on the Flesquières Ridge, making use of the former German trenches. As far as the British were concerned, the Battle of Cambrai was over. The remaining tanks were pulled back to prepare for entrainment to their winter quarters and some of the crews even went home on leave.

But no one had reckoned with German intentions. On the morning of November 30th, while the British were carrying out an orderly withdrawal, the Germans launched a major counter offensive that in many ways was just as sudden and surprising as the original British attack. The German plan was nothing less than to cut off and destroy the whole of the British forces in the salient which had been formed by their advance on Cambrai. For a while the situation was alarming, especially in the southern sector where the Germans not only succeeded in regaining lost ground but broke through the original British lines. Turning northwards they attacked the British flank and prepared to cut off the salient. The tanks that still remained in the area, an assortment of 63 of them, were quickly rounded up and sent into action at Gouzeaucourt. They made a vital contribution in the desperate battle to prevent the enemy's attacking groups from converging, recognised by Haig who stated in his Despatch: "Great credit is due to the officers and men of the Tank Brigade concerned for the speed with which they brought their tanks into action." And Fuller later commentated that "they accomplished what I have always felt to be one of the most remarkable achievements of the war".

By the time the German counter offensive petered out in a blinding snowstorm on December 7th, they had won as much ground as they had lost and achieved a more or less even balance in casualties and prisoners taken. It was by no means the worst British disaster of the year but after the great promise of victory on November 20th, the final result seemed just that much more of a bitter failure. There was a public outcry at home and even a Court of Enquiry which, needless to say, whitewashed the generals and put most of the blame on the junior officers, NCOs and men. But this time, at least, the tanks could not be blamed. They had achieved a brilliant initial success which no one could deny. They had suffered for it as well, particularly during their return to battle after the German counter attack. Of the 4,000 officers and men of the Tank Corps who had taken part, a total of 1,153 were killed or wounded. Less than a third of the 474 tanks returned to base and all of them required extensive repairs. In fact, few of them saw action again for the following year the Mark IV was superseded by the more efficient and more heavily armoured Mark V.

In spite of everything, the tanks had finally proved what they could do if used intelligently. The Battle of Cambrai was a turning point in the history of warfare. As Winston Churchill later replied to the question of what else the generals could have done, other than wage their fruitless war of attrition in Flanders and elsewhere: "I answer, pointing to the Battle of Cambrai, this could have been done. This in many variants, this in larger and better forms ought to have been done."

CHAPTER SIX

Tank versus Tank

It was inevitable that the time would come when the Germans, however belatedly, started to build tanks of their own. During the early months of 1918, stories began to trickle through from intelligence reports and the statements of captured prisoners that the Germans were building a monster tank, much larger and heavier than the British machines. In a very small way they had already used tanks in battle—a few Mark IVs captured in the Battle of Cambrai and manned by German crews. Now these tanks were withdrawn from the front line and used for training the newly formed German Panzer Corps.

The year had not started well for the Allies. The exhausting battles in Flanders had taken their toll so that the total number of French, British and Belgian divisions had been reduced from 178 at the beginning of 1917 to 164 by 1918. In addition, the strength of each British division had been reduced from thirteen to ten battalions, inevitably affecting their fighting efficiency. It was true that powerful reinforcements were expected from the United States, following her entry into the war during the previous April, but by March 1918 only four American divisions had arrived and these had not yet entered the front line. Apart from the general weariness of the troops, the Allies were hampered by internal friction among their generals and political leaders. In 1917 the British, who had taken the main offensive role, had a frontage of 100 miles as against 325 miles held by the French. After some argument, in which the French at first demanded that the British line be extended by a further 55 miles, Haig agreed to take on another 25 miles and no more, threatening to resign if overruled by the newly-formed Allied Supreme War Council. He had his way, so that by the early spring of 1918 the British with 58 divisions held 125 miles of the front while 99 French divisions took charge of 300 miles. The disparity was less than it seemed because half of the French line was of secondary importance. But the bickering between the two armies did little for morale, which was already at a low ebb.

The Germans on the other hand had reason for confidence. The collapse of Russia towards the end of 1917 had released divisions from the eastern front, to the point where the balance in the west was altered in their favour. Whereas at the beginning of 1917 the Germans were outnumbered nearly three to two by the Allies—129 divisions against 178—the situation a year later on the Western Front was 192 German divisions against 164 of the Allies. Realising the enormous potential of the United States once the build-up of her forces got really under way, Ludendorff decided to launch a major offensive in the hope of securing a quick victory and favourable peace terms. It was to begin on March 21st, initially against the 54-mile southern sector of the British line between the Oise and Sensée rivers.

By that time the British Tank Corps had been expanded to fourteen battalions with an establishment of 24,000 officers and men. The former lettered titles had been changed to numerical ones—A Battalion becoming the 1st Battalion and so on—but letters were used for companies which became A, B and C companies of each battalion. Two new tanks had been developed for use in the 1918 campaign. The heavy Mark V was again similar in shape to the Mark IV but with a much improved performance, reliability and manoeuvrability. A larger 150hp Ricardo engine gave it an increased speed of 4.6mph and new epicyclic gears designed by Wilson enabled it to be driven and steered by one man, a tremendous asset in battle since the rest of the crew could concentrate on firing the guns. The thickness of armour was increased from a maximum of 12mm on the Mark IV to 14mm, while the Hotchkiss replaced the Lewis machine guns. The worst feature of the new design was in placing the radiator inside the tank, for although it provided a more efficient cooling system than in previous models, it severely reduced ventilation for the crew.

The same problem was also found in the other new tank which came into service in 1918, the light Medium Mark A Whippet which had originally been designed by Tritton at the end of 1916. This was intended for exploiting a breach in the enemy's line rather than crossing trenches and was armed only with light machine guns. It had a speed of over 8mph and a range of 80 miles compared with the Mark V's 45 miles. The tracks did not go all round the hull but around a chassis on which the engine room and fighting turret were mounted, so that its shape was reminiscent of the original 'Little Willie'. Its crew consisted of a commander and two men. While the role of the Mark V in battle was comparable to the heavy cavalry, the Whippet formed the light cavalry for skirmishing purposes.

The French had also developed tanks of their own. The heavy St Chamond (23 tons) and the medium Schneider (14 tons) had first been used in action in April and May 1917 but the results were disappointing. Both were virtually armoured cabins mounted on adaptations of the Holt tractor. Four hundred of each were built but they had poor cross country performance and limited fighting capacity. By 1918 the French had developed a light Renault tank of 6½ tons which was much more successful. It was relatively cheap to build and after its debut in battle later in the year, large numbers were ordered.

Just as the British High Command had underrated the machine gun, so the Germans underrated the tank. The real shock had come in the Battle of Cambrai when the Mark IV, its thicker armour impervious to bullets, showed how easily trench defences could be assaulted. The fact that there were flaws in the British plan which failed to take advantage of the breakthrough could not disguise the potential of this new form of warfare. The Daimler Motor Company had already designed a tank designated the A7V and now it was hurried into production. But in reality it was too late. There was not sufficient time for proper development work to be carried out. Only ten of these tanks were ready to take part in the March offensive. Later in the campaign, five more A7Vs became available—making up the total of 15 built by the Germans before the war ended—and about 25 captured British tanks were also used. They were too few for the Panzer Corps to make any great impact in the battles of 1918.

Although clumsy and in many ways badly designed, the A7V was a monstrous vehicle that could strike terror in the hearts of the unprotected British infantry. It weighed nearly 40 tons and carried a crew of sixteen, sandwiched into a space 24ft long by 10½ft wide. Heavy 30mm armour plate that could withstand a direct frontal hit from field guns at long range extended right down over the tracks so that the tank looked like a huge tortoise. It had an impressive speed of up to 8mph and bristled with six machine guns and one 57mm gun, the equivalent of a 6pdr. Because of the underhanging tracks it had a very limited ground clearance and was unable to cross large trenches or shelled ground. The armour over the drivers' cabin was too thin to provide much protection and numerous crevices in the plating made it highly susceptible to bullet splash. Its most interesting feature, not yet incorporated in British or French tanks, was the provision of sprung tracks to give a smoother ride on flat ground.

Tanks played little part in the opening stages of the great German offensive, for which new techniques had been devised. The artillery bombardment was started without previous 'registration' fire so that it came as a sudden, paralysing blow, increased by the use of a high proportion of gas shell. Having learned the value of a surprise attack, just as the British had at Cambrai, the German infantry began to move forwards almost immediately, followed by the second line reserves who were thus on hand when they were needed. Instead of advancing on an even front and waiting while centres of resistance were overcome, the German infantry had been trained in new infiltration tactics to follow along the line of least resistance. They were aided by a thick mist which covered the 54 mile battle front on the morning of March 21st. The front line defences of the British Third and Fifth Armies were overrun even before the defenders were aware of it. With 64 divisions taking part against 29 British infantry divisions and three cavalry divisions, the Germans advanced rapidly and by the end of the first day had breached the battle zone in several sectors. The British front was in danger of collapse.

Meanwhile the bulk of the British tank battalions, comprising at that time 324 Mark IVs and about fifty Whippets, had been distributed in three main groups some ten miles behind the front. As a defensive scheme in preparation for the expected German offensive, most of them were hidden in concealed positions, the idea being that they would emerge 'like savage rabbits from their holes' to ambush any German units penetrating the battle zone. In view of their slow speed and inability to move quickly to the areas where most needed, it was not a role particularly suited to tanks. The whole

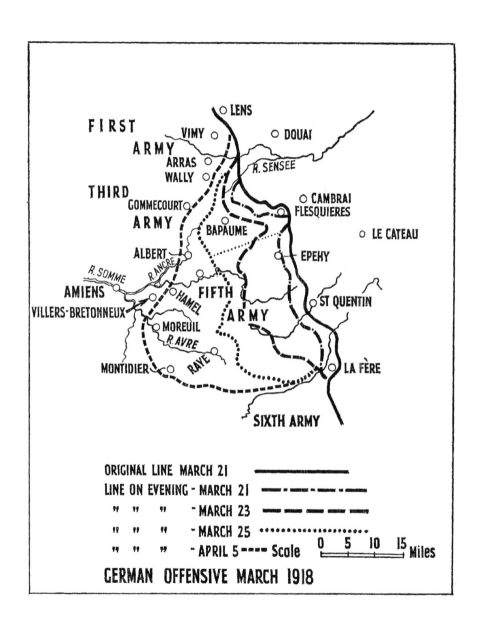

ORIGINAL LINE MARCH 21
LINE ON EVENING - MARCH 21
  "   "   "   - MARCH 23
  "   "   "   - MARCH 25
  "   "   "   - APRIL 5 ---- Scale

0   5   10   15
Miles

GERMAN OFFENSIVE MARCH 1918

initial period of the battle became known to the Tank Corps, somewhat sarcastically, as 'Savage Rabbits'.

During the days of crisis that followed, pockets of these tanks did invaluable work in preventing the British retreat from becoming a rout. The most critical moments came on March 26th when the Germans, having advanced nearly 20 miles on a front of about 40 miles, strenuously attempted to make the final breakthrough. It was on that day that the Whippets came into action for the first time, preventing the enemy from taking advantage of a four mile gap which had opened up in the Third Army's defences at Serre, and it also marked a momentous decision by the Allies to appoint General Foch as Commander-in-Chief of the Allied Armies to co-ordinate the operations of the French and British forces. By nightfall, due in no small part to counter attacks by both light and heavy tanks, the immediate danger had passed. The Germans had made the greatest advances since the war had become deadlocked in trench fighting but could not keep up their supplies across the devastated ground. North of the Somme the front became stabilised by the reformed British defences and little further ground was lost. Southwards, the Germans advanced over the next two days until they were nearly at Villers-Bretonneux, only ten miles from Amiens. It was at Amiens, with its vitally important railway junction, that the British and French armies met and it was largely with the intention of breaking between them that the German offensive had been launched. But the British withdrawal in this area had been conducted largely to conform to the position taken by the French. Although the Germans had driven a wedge nearly forty miles deep in the British lines towards Amiens and taken about 80,000 prisoners, they had for the time being shot their bolt.

Between March 28th and April 18th the Germans switched their attack to other sectors of the front, first at Arras and then, when that failed, towards Hazebrouck in Flanders. Here, the British were forced to abandon the ground that had been won so dearly at Passchendaele the previous year but managed to check the German advance by withdrawing to a shorter line at Ypres.

On April 24th the Germans made a renewed effort in the south by a surprise attack on Villers-Bretonneux. For the first time in the war they decided to use tanks to spearhead the attack, bringing up twelve A7Vs secretly to the front under cover of darkness. It was at Villers-Bretonneux, on high ground overlooking the Somme valley with the rooftops and cathedral spire of Amiens clearly visible beyond, that the first confrontation between tanks took place.

The German attack began early in the morning with an intensive bombardment of high explosive and gas shells. When this lifted at about 6am the troops in the British forward trenches prepared themselves for the infantry assault. But it was not the expected stormtroopers who came through the thick fog which persistently clung over the Somme country. Instead, there came the looming, fearsome shapes of German tanks, the noise of their approach having been drowned by the roar of shellfire. They created the same kind of havoc in the forward trenches as the British tanks had done at

Cambrai. With no antitank weapons to combat these monsters, the British troops either ran or surrendered. In the words of the British Official History, 'wherever tanks appeared the British line was broken'. A three mile gap was speedily opened for the oncoming stormtroopers. By the time the morning fog had lifted, the Germans had captured Villers-Bretonneux and the leading tank was already lumbering on towards the village of Cachy. The situation was desperate.

It so happened that lying up in the wood between Villers-Bretonneux and Cachy were three Mark IVs, appropriately enough the No. 1 Section of A Company of the 1st Tank Battalion, commanded by Captain J. C. Brown, MC. Two of these were female tanks, armed only with machine guns, but the third, under the command of Lieutenant F. Mitchell, was a male tank armed with 6pdrs. The section had been overwhelmed by the earlier gas shelling, which had disabled some of the crews, but the three tank commanders were given orders to proceed to the Cachy switch line and hold it at all costs. The story was described later by Lieutenant Mitchell.

"As the wood was still thick with gas we wore our masks. Whilst cranking up a third member of my crew collapsed and I had to leave him behind propped up against a tree trunk. A man was loaned to me by one of the females, bringing the crew, including myself, up to six instead of the normal eight. Both my first and second drivers had become casualties so the tank was driven by the third driver, whose only experience of driving was a fortnight's course at Le Tréport (the base camp)."

As Mitchell had previously reconnoitred the ground near Cachy and was most familiar with the lie of the land, he led the way. Captain Brown rode with him.

"We left at 8.45am and after a while took off our gas masks. We zigzagged undamaged through a very heavy barrage, reaching the switch line at about 9.30am. An infantryman jumped out of a trench in front of my tank and waved his rifle agitatedly. I slowed down and opened the flap. 'Look out, there are Jerry tanks about,' he shouted. This was the first intimation we had that the Germans were using tanks. I gazed ahead and saw three weirdly shaped objects moving towards the eastern edge of Cachy, one about 400 yards away, the other two being much farther away to the south. Behind the tanks I could see lines of advancing infantry.

"At this point Captain Brown left my tank, apparently to warn the females. I turned right and threading my way between the small isolated trenches that formed the Cachy switch line, went in the direction of Cachy. I was travelling more or less parallel to the nearest German tank and my left hand gunner began to range on it. The first shots went beyond but he soon ranged nearer. I noticed no reply from the German tank. There was still a mist overhead but the view on the ground was fairly clear and I was able to use the forward Lewis gun against the German infantry.

"Halfway to Cachy I turned round as the two females were patrolling the other part of the switch line. My attention was now fully fixed on the German tank nearest to me, which was moving slowly. The right-hand gunner, Sergeant J. R. McKenzie, was firing steadily at it, but as I kept continually zigzagging and there were many shellholes, accurate shooting was difficult.

"Suddenly there was a noise like a storm of hail beating against our right wall and the tank became alive with splinters. It was a broadside of armour piercing bullets from the German tank. The crew lay flat on the floor. I ordered the driver to go straight ahead and we gradually drew clear, but not before our faces were splintered. Steel helmets protected our heads.

"A few minutes later I saw Captain Brown out in the open running towards my tank. I stopped. He told me that one of the females had been hit by a shell and had dropped a wounded man in a trench, whom he asked me to pick up. We drove to the spot indicated and took the man on board. He was wounded in both legs and lay on the floor groaning during the rest of the action.

"Nearing the Bois d'Aquenne we turned once more, but owing to the driver's inexperience and the clumsiness of the secondary gears, the turn was a wide one. Captain Brown again appeared out in the open and hailed me excitedly. 'Where the hell are you going?' he yelled through the flap. 'Back towards Cachy,' I replied. He then pointed angrily in that direction and to my astonishment I saw the two females retiring from the battlefield."

In fact, both had found themselves hopelessly outgunned by the German tank. Their machine guns were of little use against the thick armourplating of the enemy, and although they used their greater manoeuvrability to try to find a chink in the opponent's armour, both were holed and forced to withdraw. Mitchell's was the only tank left, against three of the enemy.

"I continued carefully on my route in front of the switch line. The left hand gunner was now shooting well. His shells were bursting very near to the German tank. I opened a loophole at the top side of the cab for better observation and when opposite our opponent, we stopped. The gunner ranged steadily nearer and then I saw a shell burst high up on the forward part of the German tank. It was a direct hit. He obtained a second hit almost immediately lower down on the side facing us and then a third in the same region. It was splendid shooting for a man whose eyes were swollen by gas and who was working his gun single handed, owing to shortage of crew.

"The German tank stopped abruptly and tilted slightly. Men ran out of a door at the side and I fired at them with my Lewis gun. The German infantry following behind stopped also. It was about 10.20am.

"The other two German tanks now gradually drew nearer and seemed to be making in my direction. We kept shooting at the nearer one, our shells bursting all round it, when suddenly both tanks slowly withdrew and disappeared in the direction of Hangard."

And so history was made. Tank had met tank in a gun battle, and the British had won. It was more than a mere duel, however. While the tanks had been thus engaged, the British infantry had been forced back from Villers-Bretonneux, suffering heavy casualties, and held only the southern half of the Cathy

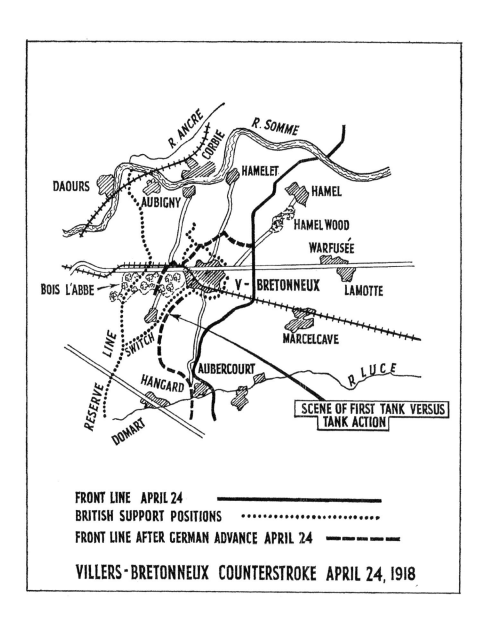

SCENE OF FIRST TANK VERSUS
TANK ACTION

FRONT LINE   APRIL 24   ————————————
BRITISH SUPPORT POSITIONS   ••••••••••••••••••••••
FRONT LINE AFTER GERMAN ADVANCE APRIL 24   — — — — — —

VILLERS-BRETONNEUX COUNTERSTROKE APRIL 24, 1918

Top: A German tank in action, June 1918.

Above: At last the Germans introduce tanks of their own, the massive A7V which weighed twice as much as British tanks and carried a crew of 18, packed like sardines in an area 24ft long and 10½ft wide, part of which was also taken up by the two 100hp engines.

Above: Infantry follow a tank into action, under cover of a smoke screen.
Below: Result of the first tank versus tank action at Villers-Bretonneux on April 24th, 1918, when one of the three attacking German tanks was disabled.

Below: A British Mark V trundles down the street of a demolished village in the Battle of Hamel which began on July 4th in appreciation of American Independence Day and the fact that American troops were to take part for the first time.

Top: The Mark V Star was an elongated version of the Mark V which could carry up to 25 troops in addition to its crew of eight. Note the semaphore signalling device on top, for communication between tanks in battle.

Above: French Renault light tanks resting after an attack near Grisolles on the River Aisne on July 28th, 1918.

Top: Renault tanks on their way to the front.

Above: Mark V tanks of the 9th Battalion during the British offensive on August 8th, 1918.

Top left: A tank comes to rescue another which has slipped over the edge of a flooded road between Ignacourt and Cayeux in the Luce Valley during the Battle of Amiens.

Left: Even by 1918, carrier pigeons were still being used for sending messages back from tanks in battle.

Above: Tank officers examine a captured anti-tank gun during the Battle of Amiens. This gun fired a cartridge about five inches long with a half inch bore.

Above: Tanks advancing through a village on August 10th, 1918, passing a wrecked Canadian ammunition wagon and German prisoners.

Below: British Mark Vs going into action between Amiens and Bouchoir on the Somme.

Above: Tanks lined up and waiting to advance.

Below: The remains of a Whippet blown up by a direct shell hit at Villers-Bretonneux.

Top left: A Whippet tank on its way to co-operate with the New Zealand Brigade in the capture of Biefvillers on August 24th, 1918.

Centre left: Tank and infantry take a rest before advancing.

Left: A Mark V helps Canadian infantry in routing out a German machine gun post near Lichons on August 18th, 1918.

Top: British armoured cars on reconnaissance at Biefvillers during the Second Battle of the Somme.

Above: New Zealand troops examine a captured anti-tank rifle after their successful attack on Grevillers on August 25th, 1918.

Above: Battle traffic at Grevillers after its capture by the New Zealand and 37th Divisions.

Below: A tank embedded in the marsh during the Battle of the Scarpe, August 29th, 1918.

Above: A tank brings in prisoners carrying a wounded man near Moeuvres at the start of the assault on the Hindenburg Line on September 27th, 1918.

Below: Mark V tanks carrying fascines, moving up to the Hindenburg Line.

Top: British and French tanks on their way by train to the repair yards at Teneur.

Above: Salvaging parts from a tank put out of action in battle.

Top right: The Tank Corps Central Workshops at Teneur, where the vital work went on of preparing tanks for battle and salvaging those hit by enemy fire.

Centre right: Chinese riveters at work in the Central Workshops at Teneur.

Right: A Mark IV fitted with an elongated 'tadpole tail' to assist crossing very wide trenches.

Top: The Mark VII was designed in 1917 but superseded by the more powerful Mark VIII which, however, was produced too late to take part in the war.

Above: The Mark V Two Stars was fitted with a 225hp Ricardo engine and was better proportioned than the Mark V Star, but only one of the 300 ordered was delivered before the end of the war.

switch with the threat of being outflanked by the enemy who had advanced into the Bois d'Aquenne.

"These trenches", states the history of the Worcester Regiment, "were as yet intact although like the other trenches they were certain to be mere death traps if attacked by tanks. Presently help came. Three British tanks appeared in rear and came forward along the southern edge of the Bois d'Aquenne just as a hostile tank bore down to attack the Devon trenches. (Held by two companies of the Devonshire Regiment.) A fight ensued between the clumsy monsters. The first two British tanks, weak female machines, were knocked out but the big male tank, which came up behind them, attacked the German tank, secured three direct hits, and forced it into a sandpit, where the German tank was ditched and abandoned by its crew."

Not only did the appearance of the British tanks at such a critical moment have an encouraging effect on the hard pressed infantry, but by forcing the German tanks to withdraw, they put the German infantry at risk from tank attack. And that is precisely what happened. It so happened that during the battle between British and German tanks, seven Whippets of Captain T. R. Price's company of the 3rd Battalion were lying up in a wood only three miles behind Cachy. The pilot of a British reconnaissance aircraft had seen the German infantry gathering to attack and dropped a message to inform Price that he might be able to take them unawares if he could get there in time.

The seven tanks roared off, led by Price, and found the enemy troops spread out across a hollow. Had any of the German tanks been present, they would have been more than a match for the little Whippets, armed only with machine guns. But the Germans had withdrawn after the encounter with Mitchell's Mark IV. With nothing to stop him Price deployed his tanks in line, about 50 paces apart, and charged at full speed across the open, undulating country that was so ideal for tank movement. What followed was a massacre. The surprised enemy troops were mown down by the relentless fire of 14 blazing machine guns. Some of them unwisely sought refuge in shellholes and were crushed to death as the tanks ran over them. Turning round at the other side of the hollow the Whippets made a second terrible run, at the end of which their tracks were literally 'covered in blood and human remains'. At least 400 of the enemy were killed, for the loss of one tank which, against Price's orders, had gone on too far and shown itself above the skyline where it was knocked out by a German field gun battery placed near Hangard.

So demoralised were the enemy that their attack on Cachy never materialised. Later that night and in the early hours of April 25th, in a daring moonlight attack that succeeded against all odds, Australian troops of the 13th and 15th Brigades recaptured Villers-Bretonneux and from then on remained guardians of the shattered town. The German drive towards Amiens was halted.

By mid May the Tank Corps strength had been built up to include 387

Mark IVs, 129 Mark Vs and 82 Whippets. The Mark Vs were arriving at the rate of about fifty a week. Now that the German offensive had been halted it was decided by the British High Command to undertake a small scale attack to test the state of German morale and also to try out the Mark Vs in battle before launching a major assault. The objective chosen was a ridge north of Villers-Bretonneux on which stood the remains of Hamel village. This meant an advance of only one and a half miles across open country but capture of the ridge would greatly improve the defensive position south of the Somme. The front line at this sector was held by the Australian Corps under the command of General Monash and the Australian troops, remembering the fiasco of the Bullecourt attack a year before, had little confidence in tanks. It was agreed therefore to rely mainly on the tanks and risk as few infantry as possible. Only ten infantry battalions (including four companies of American infantry) were employed on the attack frontage of $3\frac{1}{2}$ miles with 60 fighting tanks.

The attack started at 3.10am on July 4th without any preliminary artillery bombardment, following the Cambrai pattern, and came as a complete surprise to the Germans. The sound of the tanks moving up was drowned in normal harassing fire and they were already heading for the German lines when at zero hour the creeping barrage opened with a crash and only four minutes later lifted and rolled on. Because of the doubts still held by the Australians it had been planned for the tanks to follow the first wave of infantry but the Mark Vs soon began to draw ahead and led the way. The battle was over in less than two hours with all the objectives gained. More than 1,500 prisoners were taken, 2 field guns and 171 machine guns, apart from 200 machine guns knocked out by the tanks. The Australian casualties were only 672 and the American 134, while all but two of the tanks reached the objective, one being hit by the enemy and one by the British artillery. Thirteen of the tank crews were wounded but none killed.

The little Battle of Hamel was a brilliant success, unique in the Great War for its rapidity, brevity and completeness. It finally convinced the High Command of the tremendous offensive power of armour and paved the way for the decisive battle of the war, at Amiens on August 8th.

CHAPTER SEVEN

The Battle of Amiens

The great German offensives of the spring and summer of 1918, launched in the hope of a decisive victory before the build up of American forces tilted the odds against them, had succeeded in gaining some ground. But, just as the Allies had learned from such bitter experience before them, the impetus of their attacks ran down because of lack of mobility and transportation. After being stopped short of Amiens by the British, they turned their attention farther to the south, against the French. On July 15th they launched their last big attack, on either side of Rheims. The French front line was only lightly held and swung back, enabling the Germans to make their nearest advance to Paris. Then three days later the French, in the only mass assault by tanks that they made during the war, using over 200 medium heavy and 150 light tanks, counter attacked the enemy's exposed flank. The Germans fell back four miles across the Marne before they managed to reform their line. But now they found themselves in a dangerously exposed salient, facing the British to the north from Ypres to Amiens, the French in the centre as far as the River Aisne, and the Americans from the Aisne to Verdun. The Allies began to plan for a major offensive in September which, by attacking at the southern and northern ends of the line while the French kept up a steady pressure in the centre, would encircle the entire German army. It was a reasonable strategy. But victory was to come about in a different way.

Although the German advance towards Amiens had been halted and Hamel and Villers-Bretonneux retaken, Haig was concerned that the enemy still held the important railways east of Amiens which linked through the French lines with Paris. When at a conference towards the end of July the Allied Commander-in-Chief, General Foch, asked the British, French and American Armies to undertake a series of limited local offensives, Haig put forward the idea of an operation east and south-east of Amiens to disengage the town and the vital railway link. This meant an advance to a maximum of seven miles on the Albert to Montdidier front, held mainly by Rawlinson's Fourth Army. The plan was agreed by Foch, while the French and American armies were given the role of freeing other strategic railways farther to the south and east. But these attacks would depend largely on the progress made by the British, whose offensive was the most important and considered more likely to achieve the best results. If successful, the advance could be continued in a second attack towards the St Quentin-Cambrai line and the elaborate Hindenburg defences which had briefly been broken at the Battle of Cambrai the year before. Twenty miles behind the Hindenburg Line lay the great railway centre of Maubeuge which was the key position to the whole German system of lateral communication, the only means of supplying and maintaining the German forces on the Champagne front to the south. If the British could penetrate that far, those forces would be completely cut off from the German armies operating in Flanders. In such an event it was tentatively suggested that the French and American armies could attack in a converging direction towards Mezières, part of the same railway system. But this was looking very far ahead and for the moment, plans for such exploitation were only vaguely sketched. The disengagement of Amiens was the immediate objective. August 8th was the date selected for the attack. Although no one realised it at the time, that day was to mark the turning point of the entire war.

The British Fourth Army at this time consisted of thirteen infantry divisions, including the Canadian and Australian Corps, and three divisions of the Cavalry Corps which contained all but five of the 28 regular cavalry regiments. Opposing them on the German front were six divisions of the German Second Army under General von der Marwitz, with another six divisions held in reserve within a three hour march of the final Allied objective, a line of villages running across the Santerre plain from Mericourt on the south bank of the Somme to Hangest, a mile to the south of the Amiens to Roye road. The frontage of the British attack was ten miles while in a subsidiary operation, two divisions of the French First Army were to attack in the general direction of Roye. But the most important part of the British plan was that the attack should be spearheaded by tanks. The success of the Battle of Hamel and that of the French on July 18th prompted the idea, only now on a much larger scale. The whole available strength of the Tank Corps had been concentrated on the Fourth Army sector of the front and all were to be used. Nine heavy battalions, 324 Mark V fighting tanks, would lead the attack while two light battalions, 96 Whippets, were to exploit any breakthrough with the Cavalry Corps. A further 42 tanks were held in mechanical reserve, 120 used as supply tanks, and 22 as gun-carriers, making a grand total of 604, the largest number ever gathered together in any one place.

The main assault was to be made south of the Somme by the Australian Corps to the left and the Canadian Corps to the right, allotted respectively the V Tank Brigade with the 17th Armoured Car Battalion and the IV Tank Brigade. Their objectives extended to about four miles into the German defences. Then the Cavalry Corps, with the Whippets of the III Tank Brigade under its command, was to pass through and take the remaining two to three miles as far as the former French front line which they were to hold until relieved by the infantry of the two assault corps. Meanwhile, the Fourth Army's III Corps was to make a more limited advance north of the Somme, standing firm around Albert. For this purpose they were allotted the 10th Battalion of the II Tank Brigade, its only remaining unit since the other battalions had been temporarily moved across to help with the main attack.

On the right of the front, the French XXXI Corps had a similar task to out-flank the Montdidier defences, only without the aid of tanks.

Since their advance across the Santerre plain in March the Germans had not had time to prepare much of a trench system that was likely to impede either the tanks or the infantry. Therefore the British attack was to be made on the Cambrai pattern, without a preliminary artillery bombardment but under the protection of a creeping barrage. The heavy Mark V and Mark V Star tanks, strung out along the front of the attack, were to lead the infantry into action and then fight individually in an infantry support role since even by that time no effective communication between tanks in battle had been devised. Zero hour was fixed for 4.20am on August 8th, an hour before sunrise. The whole plan depended on the utmost secrecy for any previous warning would have made it a simple matter for General von der Marwitz to scotch the offensive by pulling back the main body of his men and then counter attacking when the impetus of the British attack had run down, just as the French Fourth Army had done on July 15th. But secrecy was not easy to achieve considering the vast amount of men and equipment that had to be brought up to the front in preparation for the attack. There was little scope for concealment in the area of open ground east of Amiens, under direct observation from the German-held hills south of the Luce, where the Australian and Canadian Corps were to make the main attack on an eight mile front. Each Corps was to employ four divisions, with one division each held in reserve further back. They had a combined allotment of nearly 1,000 guns, ranging from 8in howitzers to 60pdrs. In addition each corps was allocated a brigade of four battalions of heavy tanks, consisting of 144 fighting tanks and 24 carrying tanks, making a total of 336 tanks, while the Australians also had a battalion of armoured cars. The Cavalry Corps not only had to bring up 23 mounted regiments but was also responsible for two battalions of Whippet tanks, with 48 in each. This great mass of men, horses, guns, tanks and ammunition had to be concentrated into an area of a few square miles.

As complete concealment was out of the question, Rawlinson and Haig devised an elaborate bluff to give the impression that an attack in Flanders was imminent. Indications were given that the Canadian Corps had been transferred to the Second Army for that purpose, and to aid the deception, two Canadian battalions were actually put into line on the Kemmel front where such an attack might have been expected. The RAF contributed by increasing their flying activities over Kemmel and constructing dummy airfields. Meanwhile, a second part of the bluff was to move an Australian brigade to take over the four miles of trenches held by the French south of Villers-Bretonneux. This accounted for the presence of the Australians in the sector and appeared to be a defensive measure designed to assist the French while they concentrated for an attack in the Marne area. A rumour was also put around to explain the appearance of the Canadians in Amiens, that they were later to relieve the Australians.

German Intelligence was duly deceived and suspected no more than front line skirmishing. But as the time for the great attack drew nearer, it was the arrival of the tanks which caused the biggest threat to secrecy. During the three nights beforehand they were moved up in easy stages, either camouflaged or hiding out in woods by day. German aircraft were so harried by the RAF that they could not reconnoitre behind the British front. But at night, even though they moved as quietly as possible in low gear, there was no way of preventing the noise made by so many tanks. This was reported on several occasions by German troops holding the front line, but the German High Command ridiculed such nervousness, having become indifferent to tank alarms after so many previous cries of 'wolf, wolf' which had proved unfounded.

By the morning of August 7th, the main assault force had been assembled within two or three miles of the enemy lines. The eight infantry divisions were well hidden in trenches, the Australians in those specially dug for the purpose east of Amiens while the Canadians had moved into the lines vacated by the French. The tanks had been moved into woods and ruined farm buildings, the noise of their final approach hidden by Handley Page bombers of the RAF whose raids were synchronised with the tank movements. Villers-Bretonneux on the eve of battle seemed strangely quiet and deserted. General Sir John Monash, commanding the Australian Corps, had forbidden forward reconnaissance by his officers, insisting that they rely on air photographs. But the scene was deceptive. As Monash later wrote, after inspecting the forward area: "It was only when the explosion of a stray enemy shell would cause hundreds of heads to peer out from trenches, gun-pits and underground shelters, that one became aware that the whole country was really packed thick with a teeming population carefully hidden away."

Late in the afternoon, one of these stray shells nearly ruined the whole operation. It happened to land on a carrying tank laden with petrol which was hidden in an orchard north of Villers-Bretonneux. The resulting blaze brought a deluge of shells which destroyed fourteen more tanks and set fire to a large quantity of petrol and ammunition. This might well have indicated the presence of tanks to the Germans but it was too late to do anything about it, other than to bring up replacement stores. The German gunners, after congratulating themselves, did pass on a report as to their suspicions but it was ignored by their senior commanders who had convinced themselves that the Allies were not planning an attack in this sector.

The night of August 7–8th was damp and still. It was now time for the cavalry to move up, passing through Amiens on roads strewn with sand to muffle the sound of the horses' hooves. With them came the Whippet tanks. Meanwhile the advance infantry patrols crept out of their trenches to cover the forming up of the main assault groups in no-man's land, ten phalanxes of them spread across ten miles of frontage. Shortly after 2am a single Handley Page bomber took off and began to fly up and down the line, the drone of its engines disguising the noise made by the tanks as they lumbered from their hiding places towards the front. A thick blanket of mist had drifted up the river valley which, coupled with the darkness, made it impossible to see further than a few yards. Several tanks lost their way. At 4.20am, as a glimmer in the eastern sky signalled the approach of dawn, the whole front was suddenly lit as by sheet lightning when the blast of 3,500 British and French guns heralded the start of the Battle of Amiens.

The scene was described by Lieutenant J. Robertson, commanding the Mark V tank *Oblivis Caris* of 14th Battalion, attached to the Canadian Corps 2nd Division. He wrote in his diary:

"We left our position at Villers-Bretonneux at 4.10 in order to be up with the infantry when our barrage opened up ten minutes later. Just as we reached the top of the ridge there was a terrific crash outside my bus and the port gunners staggered back. I didn't get time to worry about them for simultaneously a fierce barrage broke on the ridge. My first thought was that the enemy had been informed of the attack and I sort of wondered who would get my rum ration. We were through the muck in two minutes however, only to find ourselves lost in a curtain of mist. No sign of that tail lamp (from the tank ahead) that was to lead us so carefully. No sign of anything but a blank wall of fog and only the humming of twenty engines to indicate the presence of other tanks. Straight ahead was the best course and straight ahead we went. A confused impression of crossing a trench, then a shellhole filled with men.

"Then the lid came off. I had heard some of the record barrages on the Somme and the 'Hippodrome Orchestra', but never anything like that. Way beyond above the mist we could see the vivid flash of bursting shrapnel. Half a minute later, Jerry started firing off what must have been every Very light in stock, sufficient to tell us he must have been completely surprised."

All around them, other tanks and small groups of infantry were also lost in the dense mist, now thickened by the smoke of battle. But most of them were able to grope their way in the right direction so that the advance, although disjointed, continued to make progress. For the defenders, there was something even more terrifying in being able to hear but not see the tanks lumbering forward until it was too late and they were right on top of them.

As the mist began to clear, a more ordered advance was achieved.

"Somewhere about 5.15 our great chance came," continued Robertson. "We had at last found touch with the main advance and came across a company of Canadians taking cover from strong machine gun fire from a harvested field. Almost as we got there one of them gave the SOS. We didn't wait to ask questions but passed through the infantry and in two minutes found ourselves right among the Boche. One lot tried to beat it for a wood but Gunner McKellars, to his huge delight, got them all. We reached a trench crowded with Jerries and all our guns got right busy. The effect of case shot in a crowded trench isn't pretty.

"All this time some machine gun had been beating a devil's tattoo on the old bus. We located the trouble and dealt with it. I looked at my watch and saw to my surprise it was only 5.45. We seemed to have lived years in those 20 minutes. However, I had to reach my first objective at 6.23 so I gave the

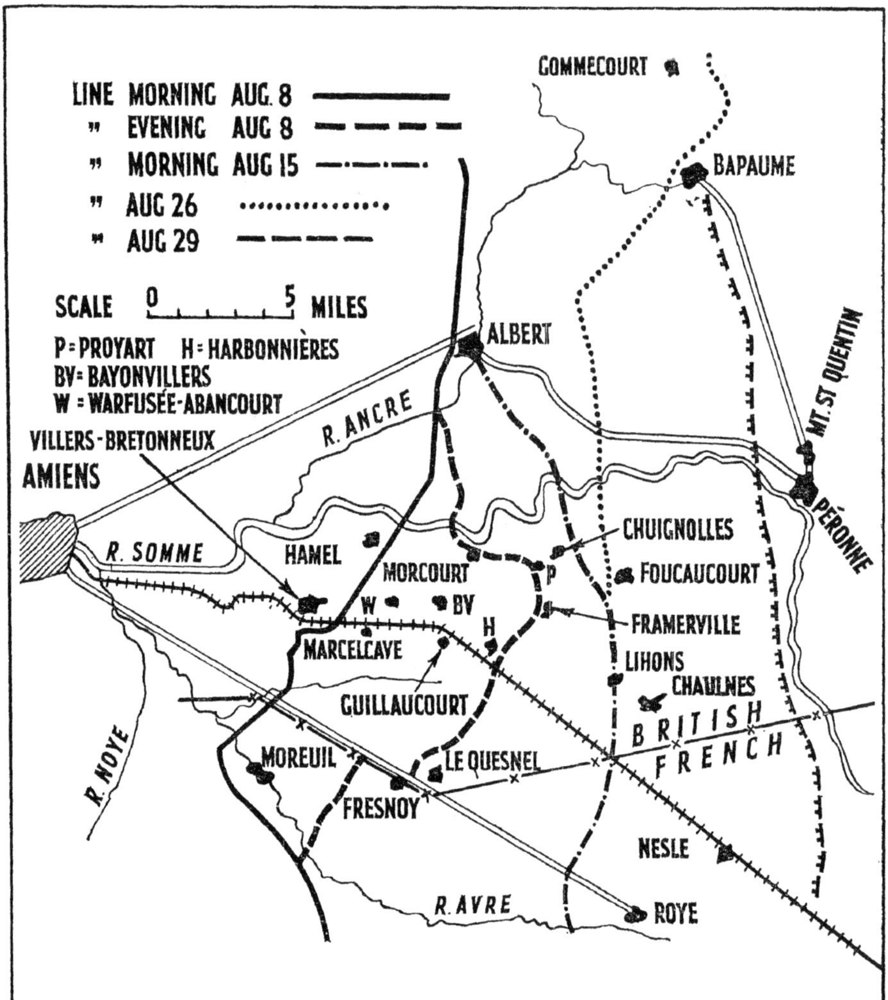

LINE MORNING AUG. 8 ——————
  "   EVENING AUG 8 — — — —
  "   MORNING AUG 15 —·—·—·—·—·
  "   AUG 26 ················
  "   AUG 29 — — — —

SCALE 0 .... 5 MILES

P = PROYART   H = HARBONNIÈRES
BV = BAYONVILLERS
W = WARFUSÉE-ABANCOURT

VILLERS-BRETONNEUX
AMIENS

GOMMECOURT

BAPAUME

MT. ST. QUENTIN

ALBERT

R. ANCRE

R. SOMME

HAMEL

MORCOURT

CHUIGNOLLES

FOUCAUCOURT

P

W   BV

H

FRAMERVILLE

MARCELCAVE

LIHONS

CHAULNES

GUILLAUCOURT

B R I T I S H

PÉRONNE

MOREUIL

LE QUESNEL

F R E N C H

R. NOYE

FRESNOY

NESLE

R. AVRE

ROYE

BATTLE OF AMIENS (AUG. 1918)

infantry the all clear and steered northeast where I had a vague idea Marcel-cave lay."

Unknown to Robertson another of his battalion's tanks, commanded by Lieutenant C. R. Percy-Eade, had just minutes before performed a remarkable feat in this village. Heavy enemy machine gun fire had been holding up the advance of the Canadian infantry. On being told this, Percy-Eade attacked the village single handed with his tank and knocked out six machine gun positions, then tackled a battery and put the gunners to flight. By the time Robertson arrived, the infantry were already mopping up and there was nothing for him to do. He decided to head back to his company's rallying point, west of Marcelcave. And then occurred, as he put it, "one of those delightful interludes which amuse everyone except those taking part".

"I took the main road as the most direct. A Hun balloon evidently spotted us and before we had gone fifty yards there was a whistle and a roar a few yards behind. Half a minute later the road in front of us went up in a cloud of smoke. The Jerry gunner had got us 'bracketed', which meant that the next shot would land between the first two. But a kink in his brain made him forget we were moving. His next shot did land in the middle of the bracket, but we had travelled 100 yards in the meantime. The gunner did the same thing four times, at which point the observer in the balloon must have died of apoplexy.

"On arrival at the rallying point, I ordered my crew into the fresh air. Steven, who had driven the approach, had been lying unconscious during the action but he revived a little when we got him out. The Canadians who had been attached as observers had spent most of the time being violently sick and collapsed completely when we dragged them out."

Everywhere along the front of attack the forward defenders were taken completely by surprise and quickly overrun. The first objective was about 3½ miles deep, the second a further three miles in the centre but only just over one mile on the wings, and then would come an exploiting advance to the third objective, eight miles from the starting line in the centre and six miles on the wings.

The Canadian Corps, advancing on a front of three divisions, secured the second objective by 11am. It had not been without losses to the tanks however. On the extreme right the 5th Battalion had a difficult obstacle in crossing the marshy stream of the Luce, where eight tanks became ditched and another seven were knocked out at close range by enemy field guns. A further 11 were lost by the time the second objective was gained, leaving only eight still in action. In the centre, 11 of the 4th Battalion tanks remained. On the left, the pace quickened as the mist cleared and 16 tanks of the 14th Battalion reached the second objective. Shortly after midday the 4th Canadian Division, led by 30 Mark V Star tanks of the 1st Battalion which were six feet longer than the Mark V and used for carrying infantry Lewis gun teams, passed through the line to advance on the third objective. Nine out of the ten tanks of A Company were knocked out by a German battery and others were lost in fierce fighting until eventually 11 tanks rallied at the objective. Over 5,000 prisoners and 161 guns had been taken in the advance by the Canadians, at a cost of only 3,500 casualties.

The advance by the Australians, delivered by two divisions, was even more spectacular. The third objective was reached by about 11am, a pace so fast that the two reserve divisions following up the attack arrived there before the remaining tanks of the 5th Tank Brigade. This was just as well since most of the crews were unconscious from fumes and carbon monoxide poisoning. The Australians captured 8,000 prisoners and 173 guns at the remarkably small cost of only 650 casualties.

On the extreme left wing, the III Corps advance north of the Somme failed after reaching the first objective, one reason being a local attack by the Germans on the previous day which had seriously hampered preparations. But south of the Somme, a considerable victory had been achieved. A gap of more than 11 miles wide and up to seven miles deep had been made in the German lines, presenting a great opportunity for exploitation. This was the moment for the Cavalry Corps and the Whippet tank battalions to push forward with the utmost speed. They did in fact move up to the third objective, passing Robertson's tank on the way.

"Streaming up the long southern track they came, headed by a regiment of Lancers. As far as the eye could reach there were trotting columns of horses while in the middle track, batteries of horse and field artillery were arriving at a gallop. A cloud of dust on the northern track heralded the Whippets, 40 of them, moving almost as fast as the artillery and going hell for leather for the next objective. The whole spectacle was one which none of us had ever expected to see in France and one we would never forget."

But having reached that point the cavalry stopped and waited. They had received no orders to advance from their headquarters which were again well to the rear. Also it became apparent that the idea of placing the Whippet tanks under the cavalry was not a success. When there was no fire, the cavalry could easily outstrip the tanks in speed. But it only needed a few surviving enemy machine guns to bring the cavalry to a complete halt, where they would have to wait for the tanks. The tanks could of course have continued forward but they were tied to the cavalry. The following comment appeared in the Weekly Tank Notes issued by Tank Corps HQ.

"By noon on the 8th August, great confusion was developing behind the enemy's lines and by this time the Whippets should have been operating five to ten miles in advance of the infantry, accentuating this demoralization. As it was, being tied down to support the cavalry, they were a long way behind the infantry advance, the reason being that, as cavalry cannot make themselves invisible on the battlefield by throwing themselves flat on the ground as infantry can, they had to retire either to a flank or to the rear to avoid being exterminated by machine gun fire."

The activities of a few individual Whippets which did push ahead were highly successful, showing what could have been done if all had been allowed a free reign to operate behind the enemy lines. The dramatic performance of one Whippet in particular, *Musical Box*, became a legend in the Tank Corps. Commanded by Lieutenant C. B. Arnold, with Driver Carney and Gunner Ribbans making up the crew this tank caused havoc amongst the enemy by penetrating nearly eight miles into the German lines, far ahead of the infantry and cavalry. It was one of 16 Whippets of B Company, 6th Battalion, which had advanced across country at zero hour towards the eastern outskirts of Villers-Bretonneux. There they passed through the British front line, where Australian infantry were advancing behind the heavy Mark V tanks, and headed due east along the Amiens-Ham railway line. The story was graphically told by Lieutenant Arnold.

"After proceeding 2,000 yards in this direction I found myself to be the leading machine, owing to the others having become ditched, etc. To my immediate front I could see more Mark V tanks being followed very closely by Australian infantry. About this time (some two hours after zero) we came under direct shell fire from a four-gun field battery, of which I could see the flashes, between Abancourt and Bayonvillers. Two Mark V tanks, 150 yards on my right, were knocked out. I saw cloud of smoke coming out of these machines and the crews evacuate them. The infantry following the heavy machines were suffering casualties from this battery."

Although close enough to the guns for the sound of each shot to be heard inside the cab, over the noise of the engine, *Musical Box* was not hit. Carney drove it behind the shelter of a belt of trees running alongside a road, then swept round and headed straight for the battery from the rear.

"On observing our appearance", Arnold wrote, "the gunners, some 30 in number, abandoned their guns and tried to get away. Gunner Ribbans and I accounted for the whole lot. I cruised forward, making a detour to the left, and shot a number of the enemy who appeared to be demoralised and were moving about the country in all directions. This detour brought me back to the railway siding NNW of Guillaucourt. I could now see other Whippets coming up and a few Mark Vs also. The Australian infantry, who followed magnificently, had now passed through the battery position which we had accounted for and were lying in a sunken road about 400 yards past the battery and slightly to the left of it. I got out of my machine and went to an Australian lieutenant and asked if he wanted any help. Whilst talking to him, he received a bullet which struck the metal shoulder title, a piece of the bullet casing entering his shoulder. While he was being dressed, Major Rycroft on horseback and Lieutenant Waterhouse and Captain Strachan of B Company, 6th Battalion, arrived and received confirmation from the Australian officer of our having knocked out the field battery."

Arnold then set off again, heading east, and after a while came upon two cavalry patrols of about a dozen men each. The first was under fire from a party of German soldiers in a field of corn which had inflicted a number of casualties. *Musical Box* surged forward, machine guns firing, and quickly put the enemy to flight. Several were killed before the remainder escaped out of sight into the corn. Shortly afterwards, Arnold saw the second patrol, swords drawn and pursuing six of the enemy.

"The leading horse was so tired that he was not gaining appreciably on the rearmost Hun. Some of the leading fugitives turned about and fired at the cavalryman, when his sword was stretched out and practically touching the back of the last Hun. Horse and rider were brought down on the left of the road. The remainder of the cavalrymen deployed to the right, coming in close under the railway embankment where they dismounted and came under fire from the enemy, who had now taken up a position on the railway bridge and were firing over the parapet, inflicting one or two casualties. I ran the machine up until we had a clear view of the bridge and killed four of the enemy with one long burst, the other two running across the bridge and so down the opposite slope out of sight.

"On our left I could see, about three quarters of a mile away, a train on fire being towed by an engine. I proceeded farther east still parallel to the railway, and approached carefully a small valley marked on my map as containing Boche hutments. As I entered the valley (between Bayonvillers and Harbonnieres) at right angles, many enemy were visible packing kits and others retiring. On our opening fire on the nearest, many others appeared from huts, making for the end of the valley, their object being to get over the embankment and so out of sight. We accounted for many of these. I cruised round, Ribbans went into one of the huts and returned, and we counted about 60 dead and wounded. There were evidences of shell fire amongst the huts, but we certainly accounted for most of the casualties counted there. I turned left from the railway and cruised across country, as lines of enemy infantry could be seen retiring. We fired at these many times at ranges of 200 to 600 yards. These targets were fleeting, owing to the enemy getting down into the corn when fired on. In spite of this, many casualties must have been inflicted as we cruised up and down for at least an hour. I did not see any more of our troops or machines after leaving the cavalry patrols already referred to."

It was by no means all plain sailing for the little Whippet. Being the only tank to get through to such a distance, far ahead of the others and the slowly advancing infantry, it was subjected to continual machine gun fire. Petrol was streaming down the sides and into the interior from riddled tins on the roof, carried for refuelling purposes on order from a distant High Command. (In his report, Arnold begged to suggest that petrol cans should no longer be carried on the outside of machines.) Petrol was running all over the inside of the cab and the fumes, combined with intense bullet splash and the great heat after being in action by this time for nearly ten hours, made it necessary for the crew to breathe through the mouthpiece of their box respirators without actually wearing them.

In every direction, the crew of *Musical Box* could see great quantities of motor and horse transport and long columns of infantry, all taking part in the great German withdrawal which was to mark the beginning of the end of the war. The tank forged in amongst them, firing sometimes at almost point blank

THE BATTLE OF AMIENS 77

range and inflicting heavy casualties. Its sudden appearance caused panic and confusion and for a while there was little return fire. But such a situation could not last for long. Realising that *Musical Box* was not part of an attacking group of tanks but only a single marauder—and one which by reaching the eastern side of the Harbonnières-Rosières road went beyond the farthest Allied objective for that day—the Germans rallied. Turning towards a small copse where many horses and men were gathered, the Whippet met the most intense rifle and machine gun fire imaginable from all sides.

"When at all possible we returned the fire, until the left hand revolver port cover was shot away. I withdrew the forward gun, locked the mounting and held the body of the gun against the hole. Petrol was still running down the inside of the back door. Fumes and heat combined were very bad. We were still moving forward and I was shouting to Driver Carney to turn about as it was impossible to continue the action, when two heavy concussions closely followed one another and the cab burst into flames. (The result of a direct hit by a field gun.)

"Carney and Ribbans got to the door and collapsed. I was almost overcome but managed to get the door open and fell out on to the ground and was able to drag out the other two men. Burning petrol was running on the ground where we were lying. The fresh air revived us and we all got up and made a short rush to get away from the burning petrol. We were all on fire. In this rush Carney was shot in the stomach and killed. We rolled over and over to try to extinguish the flames. I saw numbers of the enemy approaching from all round. The first arrival came for me with a rifle and bayonet. I got hold of this and the point of the bayonet entered my right forearm. The second man struck at my head with the butt end of his rifle, hit my shoulder and neck, and knocked me down. When I came to, there were dozens all round me and anyone who could reach me did so and I was well kicked; they were furious."

The fate of Arnold and Ribbans hung by a thread. After being viciously beaten they were taken away and stood by themselves about twenty yards clear of the crowd while an argument ensued as to whether they should be killed or taken prisoner. Eventually the latter view prevailed. The two men were marched away, given the first food they had eaten since 8.30 the previous night (it was now 3.30pm), and after treatment of their wounds were sent to prison camps. It was only after Arnold's release at the end of the war, when he was awarded the DSO, that the full story of this remarkable exploit became known.

Further demoralisation of the enemy was achieved by the exploits of 16 armoured cars of the 17th Battalion, Tank Corps, led by Lieutenant-Colonel E. J. Carter. These vehicles had been towed over the trench lines by tanks and proceeded to dash eastwards along the main St Quentin road. They shot up and killed a column of horse transport and many lorries, then blocked another road by knocking out a number of steam wagons. Two cars under Lieutenant E. Rollings charged into the village of Framerville and shot up the German advanced Corps HQ, then captured many documents including the complete defence scheme of the 20 mile stretch of the Hindenburg Line from Oise to Bellicourt which proved to be of immense value in later attacks.

By the end of the day, it was apparent that a sweeping success had been achieved. The British line had advanced over six miles while five German divisions between the Avre and the Somme were almost completely annihilated. The German Official monograph stated:

"When darkness had sunk on the 8th August over the battlefield of the Second Army, the heaviest defeat suffered by the German Army since the beginning of the war had become an accomplished fact. The total losses of the units employed in the Second Army sector can be put down as from 650 to 700 officers and 26,000 to 27,000 men. More than 400 guns and an enormous quantity of machine guns, mortars and other war material were lost. . . . More than two thirds of the total German losses was due to prisoners. Almost everywhere it was evident that German soldiers had surrendered to the enemy or thrown away rifles and equipment, abandoned trench mortars, machine guns and guns, and sought safety in flight."

The Canadians lost 3,868 casualties, of whom 1,038 were killed, while the Australians lost only 652 (83 killed), making it the cheapest victory of the war as far as the infantry were concerned. The Cavalry lost about 1,000 horses, but the heaviest price was paid by the Tank Corps who had made the success possible. Out of the 415 tanks which went into battle, 109 were knocked out by German guns and so many others were ditched or had mechanical breakdowns that only 143 were available to continue the fight the next day. Casualties totalled 79 killed, 396 wounded, and 34 missing.

Tanks had led the advance on almost every sector and had captured, single-handed sometimes, large numbers of prisoners. But their greatest achievement was in sharply reducing the number of Allied infantry casualties. A graphic illustration of this was provided in the battle report of an anonymous officer.

"Three days after the opening of the attack there was to be seen on the slopes of the valley of the Luce a notice board stating that a certain field was reserved as a British cemetery. This was the usual practice and necessary to good organisation. A cemetery was selected in each sector before a battle was to begin, in the same way as water pipes were provided and other administrative arrangements made. This particular cemetery was one of the finest ever seen. It was also empty. Not a single grave. Across it were the tracks made by tanks three days previously when this patch of ground had been in the forefront of the battle.

"The relationship between those tracks and the emptiness of the cemetery was very close. The tank is a saviour of flesh and blood, which lets the enemy spend his fury in destroying metal instead of human life. In one action at Loupart Wood, sufficient machine gun fire was directed against a tank which would have wiped out an entire infantry division had it been directed against men instead of steel."

More could have been achieved on the first day of the battle had the British not stuck so rigidly to their original plan and allowed the Whippet tanks to exploit the success. As it was, the Germans brought up reinforcements and resistance stiffened as the impetus of the attack diminished. This was only too apparent on August 10th when the Cavalry Corps had a sudden inspired vision of making a breakthrough. The 2nd and 3rd Cavalry Divisions were ordered forward, together with most of the remaining Whippet tanks. Both the cavalry and tanks suffered disastrous losses. By the following day, when the attack was suspended, only 38 tanks, including both light and heavy, were fit for action. The percentage of their losses had increased significantly as their numbers decreased, as did those of the infantry who lost over 22,000 by the end of the battle, exceeding the number of prisoners taken. The depth of the advance had by then reached ten miles, on a front extended a further 25 miles after an attack by the French First Army which, without the support of tanks, lost 24,000 men for the capture of 11,000 prisoners.

The Allies were now at the edge of the old Somme battlefields of 1916 and on the face of it were not in a much better position than then. Foch was insistent that the Fourth Army should keep up its attack, which would have squandered all the gains achieved, but Rawlinson managed to persuade both him and Haig against this. The German line was still not broken and neither did this happen during the fighting which followed as attacks were launched on other sectors of the front. In fact, by shortening their line as they slowly retreated, the Germans were actually improving their position. The great breakthrough which would encircle the German armies and 'roll up the front' as Haig envisaged never did occur. It was simply that the defeat on August 8th, described by Haig as 'the most successful operation fought by the Allied armies' and due primarily to the contribution made by the tanks, proved to the German Supreme Command that they could not win the war. Ludendorff wrote in a communiqué later captured that such an advance would have been impossible without the tanks and subsequently referred to August 8th as 'the black day of the German Army in the history of the war.' Its main effect was psychological. Faced with the failing morale of the German troops, his own confidence shattered, Ludendorff finally admitted that the war would have to be ended by negotiation and not by a German victory. On August 14th, at a conference presided over by the Kaiser, the German Secretary of State was instructed to open up peace negotiations through the intermediary of the Queen of the Netherlands. Meanwhile Ludendorff was determined that the German army should stand where it was, in order to be in a good bargaining position to obtain the most favourable peace terms. But while the admission that he could not win the war was not exactly tantamount to an admission of defeat, it was reflected in the lack of confidence and indecision of both him and his commanders in the last stages of the war.

From August 18th onwards, attacks were made against the Germans on other sectors of the front. The British Second Army advanced in Flanders to take the Outersteene Ridge. Two days later the French Tenth Army struck beyond the Oise and gained up to three miles on a 12 mile frontage. On August 21st the British Third Army attacked north of the Somme, opposite

Bapaume, with the aid of some 200 tanks, including some old Mark IVs which had just been discarded. The Fourth Army renewed its attack on August 23rd with 38 tanks, all that remained fit for action. And on August 26th the British First Army chimed in by striking against the northern hinge of the German line near Arras. As a result of this succession of short, sharp attacks the Germans were forced by September 3rd to fall back on their famous bastion, the Hindenburg Line. Apart from men killed and wounded they had lost over 70,000 prisoners to the Allies in the 26 days from August 8th. German morale was low at the front and even lower at home.

The last great event in which tanks were involved was the storming of the Hindenburg Line, which fittingly included the same part of the front near Cambrai where the tanks had so nearly succeeded the year before. The Tank Corps had nearly reached the end of its tether. During the four weeks since August 8th over 1,200 tanks had been in action, some 500 of them since August 21st, and losses had been heavy. Early in September the five tank brigades were withdrawn for refitting, when the total number of battalions was increased to 17 by the arrival from England of the 16th and the attachment of the 301st American Battalion equipped with Mark V Stars. On September 18th, 20 tanks of the 2nd Battalion were used in an attack by three corps of the Fourth Army between Epehy and Villeret to clear the approaches to the Hindenburg Line. Meanwhile as many tanks as possible, totalling about 230, were assembled for the assault on the Line itself. This was part of the general Allied offensive designed to cut off by a huge pincer movement the salient formed by the German front between Verdun and Ypres. The Allied strength on the Western Front at this time consisted of 198 operational divisions, made up of 97 French, 62 British, 25 American, 12 Belgian and 2 Italian. The Germans had 197 divisions, eleven less than on August 8th, of which 70 were opposite the British.

The attack by the right pincer arm came first, on September 26th, when the French Fourth Army and the American First Army under General John Pershing struck on both sides of the Argonne between Rheims and Verdun. Nine American divisions made the main assault on a 20 mile front with the help of just under 200 Renault light tanks manned by American crews. They fought gamely forward to a maximum distance of five miles, enthusiasm making up for an inevitable lack of experience, but as had happened so many times before they were held up by the main defence belt in the rear when the momentum began to flag. Two days later came the left pincer arm attack in Flanders by the Belgian Army, the British Second Army, and a number of French divisions, under the overall command of King Albert of Belgium. This was much more successful and the Germans were forced to withdraw well beyond Messines and the Passchendaele ridge.

Meanwhile, the British attack in the centre against the Hindenburg Line began on September 27th. The First and Third Armies struck first on a 13 mile front between Gouzeaucourt and Sauchy Lestrée in the direction of Cambrai. On the left the Canadian Corps with 15 Mark IV tanks of the 7th

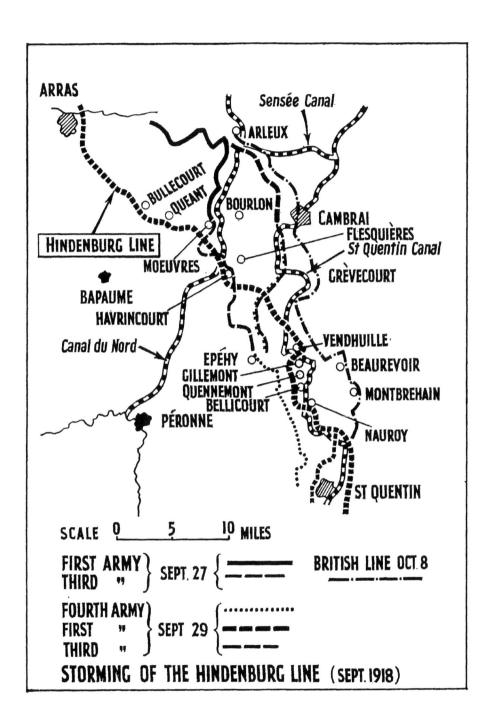

ARRAS

Sensée Canal

ARLEUX

BULLECOURT
QUEANT
BOURLON

HINDENBURG LINE

CAMBRAI
FLESQUIÈRES
St Quentin Canal

MOEUVRES

BAPAUME
HAVRINCOURT

CRÈVECOURT

Canal du Nord

VENDHUILLE
EPÉHY
GILLEMONT
QUENNEMONT
BELLICOURT

BEAUREVOIR

MONTBREHAIN

PÉRONNE

NAUROY

ST QUENTIN

SCALE 0   5   10 MILES

FIRST ARMY }
THIRD " } SEP. 27 { ━━━━   BRITISH LINE OCT. 8
━ ━ ━ ━
━ ・ ━ ・ ━ ・ ━

FOURTH ARMY }
FIRST " } SEPT 29 { ⋯⋯⋯⋯⋯
THIRD " } ━ ━ ━ ━
━ ━ ━ ━

STORMING OF THE HINDENBURG LINE (SEPT. 1918)

Battalion crossed the Canal du Nord and in a spectacular advance of four miles captured Bourlon Wood and the village on the other side. An equal success was gained by the Third Army divisions on the right which, with 38 tanks of the 11th and 15th Battalions, drove through Flesquières and reached the line of the St. Quentin Canal, only two miles southwest of Cambrai. A day later the Fourth Army, including the Australian Corps and American II Corps, launched an even bigger attack further south between Holnon and Vendhuille which included heavily fortified positions on the St Quentin Canal. Over 175 tanks were amassed for this purpose, among them the newly formed American 301st Tank Battalion with 40 Mark Vs. On the right of the Fourth Army, the French First Army continued the line of attack in the St Quentin sector.

The British attack was preceded by a heavy and continuous artillery bombardment for two days, with the intention of driving the German garrisons to take refuge in their deep dugouts and tunnels and preventing carrying parties from bringing up food and ammunition. The main weight of the attack was put on the left wing, by the Australian Corps with two American divisions, where for a stretch of three miles the St Quentin Canal ran underground. Most of the tanks, seven battalions in all including those manned by the Americans, were allocated to this sector. The remaining three battalions were used for the IX Corps attack on the right wing which involved an assault crossing of the canal where it came out into the open.

The Australian-American attack began well, led by the tanks which gained their first objectives. The deepest penetration was made the American 30th Division with 33 British tanks which succeeded in storming the main and support lines and advanced over two miles to Nauroy. But in their eagerness to push forward the Americans neglected the need for mopping up the captured ground first. The Germans had merely gone into their deep shelters, practically invulnerable to bombardment, and waited there while the shells and assault troops passed over. Then they emerged and in a merciless crossfire caught the unsuspecting Americans from behind. They were mown down in their hundreds and most of the tanks knocked out. The 5th Australian Division which should have come through to exploit the initial success had to fight hard all day to reach no farther than Nauroy. The 3rd Australian Division had an equally hard fight to take the strongly defended redoubts of Quennemont Farm, Gillemont Farm and The Knoll which were only just inside the main line, beating off fierce counter attacks with the help of other III Corps divisions.

Fortunately the IX Corps attack on the right was much more successful. In the early morning mist the 46th Territorial Division, led by the Staffordshire Brigade, had stormed the Hindenburg Main Line and then crossed the St Quentin Canal with the aid of rafts and life belts which had hastily been removed from Channel steamers. After making a detour through Bellicourt, 16 tanks of the 9th Battalion came to help the supporting brigades as they attacked and breached the Hindenburg support line. Other tanks of the 5th and 6th Battalions, including Whippets, did excellent work in helping the

32nd Division to widen the breach. By nightfall the advance had been taken to nearly four miles. This was not as far as had been hoped, but at last the great Hindenburg Line with its main and support trenches had been broken in a breach five miles wide. The only remaining fortified line was the Hindenburg Reserve or Beaurevoir Line.

On October 3rd, led by 40 tanks, the Staffordshire Brigade and the Sherwood Foresters of the 46th Division made a six mile breach in the Beaurevoir Line and two days later the 2nd Australian Division swept through to capture Montbrehain. In the course of seven days the Fourth Army had broken through the mighty German defence system at the point where it was strongest and reached the open country beyond, as had the striking wings of the First and Third Armies. Over 30,000 prisoners were taken. It was now only a matter of time. While peace negotiations were opened, the Allies kept up the pressure of their attacks. But there were few tanks left to help them. Less than 100 could be scraped together for the combined attack launched on October 8th by the Third and Fourth Armies on their whole 17 mile front southwards from Cambrai. By this time the Tank Corps had lost about one third of its fighting force of officers and men and over 800 tanks had gone to salvage, for repair if possible.

With no hope of winning the war, still the Germans continued to fight stubbornly as they slowly retreated. In open country, tanks could have been a great asset in speeding the Allied advance. But their resources were exhausted with the storming of the Hindenburg Line. As it was, when the Armistice was declared on November 11th, the British armies had only advanced about 40 miles beyond the Hindenburg Line. The last tank action took place on November 5th when eight Whippets of the 6th Battalion helped the 3rd Guards Brigade to advance past the Forest of Mormal.

Between August 8th and that last action, no less than 1,993 tanks and armoured cars had been engaged, fighting almost continuously. In his final despatch, Field-Marshal Sir Douglas Haig paid due credit to the Tank Corps:

"Since the opening of our offensive on August 8, tanks have been employed on every battlefield, and the importance of the part played by them in breaking up the resistance of the German infantry can scarcely be exaggerated. The whole scheme of the attack of August 8 was dependent upon tanks, and ever since that date on numberless occasions the success of our infantry has been powerfully assisted or confirmed by their timely arrival. So great has been the effect produced upon the German infantry by the appearance of British tanks that in more than one instance, when for various reasons real tanks were not available in sufficient numbers, valuable results have been obtained by the use of dummy tanks painted on frames of wood and canvas."

They were very different from the words used about tanks only two years before at their first appearance in battle. The tank had started as little more than the dream of a few visionaries, men who were appalled at the futility and waste of trench warfare and who fought against the bone headed stubbornness of the generals for their ideas of a better way to wage war. Now the tank had proved itself indispensable in battle. Warfare had become mechanised and would never again be the same. The tank itself was of course capable of inflicting great casualties, but not as great as those caused in the terrible earlier battles of World War I when unprotected men were slaughtered in their hundreds of thousands by machine gun fire. The infantry man had at last found a friend and in spite of the devastating power of modern weapons, casualties in battle would never again reach those proportions.

Mark I.

Opposite: This was the first tank to be made and used in action. It saw service from the Battle of the Somme in 1916 to the Battle of Arras in 1917. Although many mechanical improvements were made to later models, all the British heavy tanks used in the war followed the basic design of the Mark I.

Appendix 1

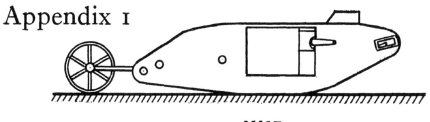

MALE

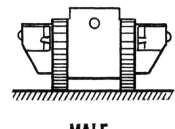

MALE

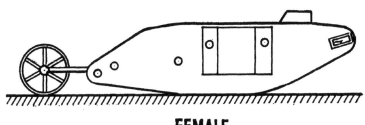

FEMALE

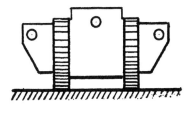

FEMALE

MARK 1

Appendix 2

MARK IV

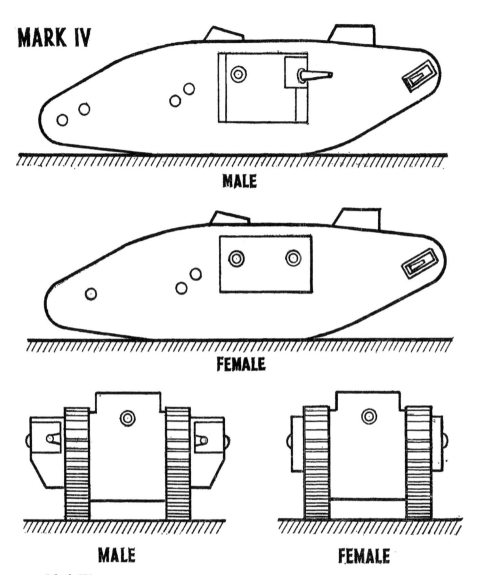

MALE

FEMALE

MALE   **FEMALE**

Mark IV.

The most widely used tank of the war and the standard fighting machine of the British Tank Corps in 1917 and 1918. A number were shipped to the Middle East for operations against the Turks.

Mark V.

Opposite: Introduced in 1918, the Mark V was the first tank capable of being driven by one man and was the combat vehicle most frequently used by the Tank Corps in the final battles of the war.

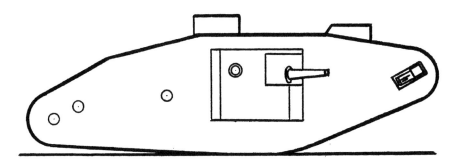

SIDE VIEW - MALE

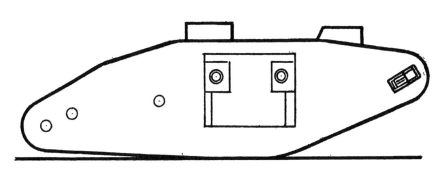

SIDE VIEW - FEMALE

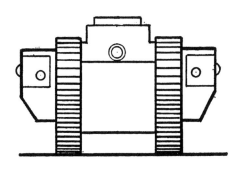 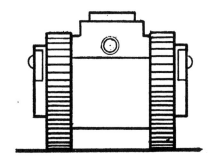

FRONT VIEW - MALE **FRONT VIEW - FEMALE**

MARK V

Appendix 4

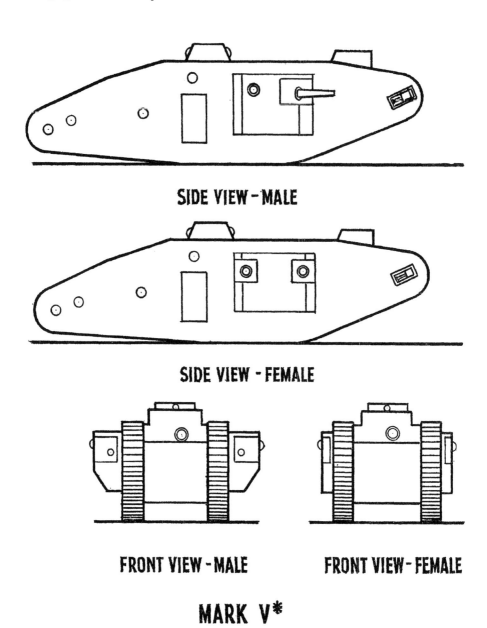

SIDE VIEW – MALE

SIDE VIEW – FEMALE

FRONT VIEW – MALE

FRONT VIEW – FEMALE

MARK V*

Mark V One Star.

This had the same mechanical arrangement as the Mark V but was six feet longer which enabled it to cross wider trenches. The extra length, which necessitated the installation of a Cardan shaft between the fly-wheel and gear-box, made it relatively slow to manoeuvre.

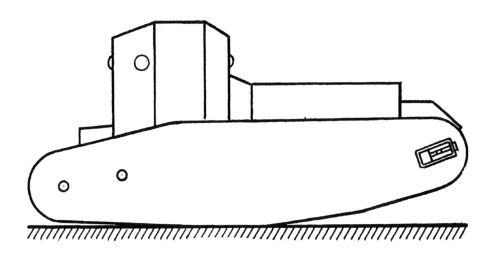

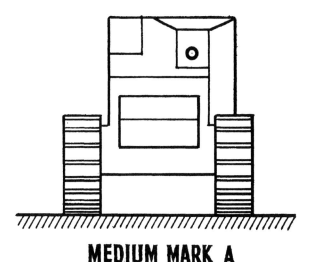

MEDIUM MARK A

Medium Mark A.

Also known as the "Whippet" or the "Chaser", the Medium Mark A was introduced in 1918 and became the standard light type machine of the Tank Corps. It required a great deal of skill to drive and the stalling of one or both engines was a common occurrence during the early stages of training.

Appendix 6

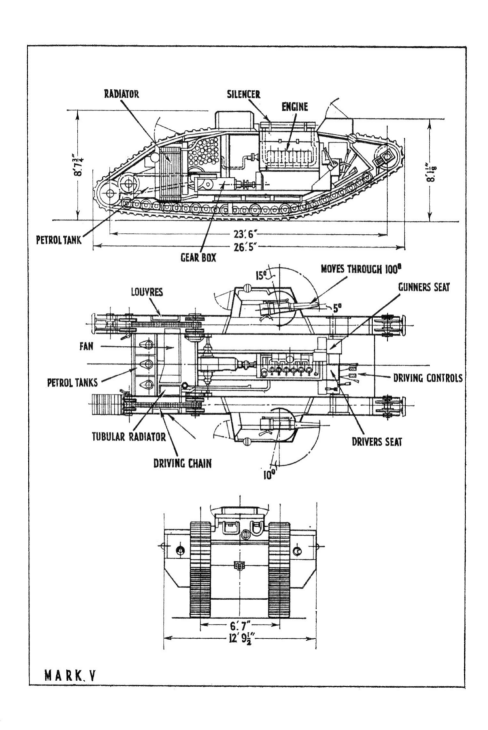

RADIATOR SILENCER ENGINE

8'7¾"

8'1⅛"

PETROL TANK

23'6"

26'5"

GEAR BOX

MOVES THROUGH 100°

15°

LOUVRES

GUNNERS SEAT

5°

FAN

PETROL TANKS

DRIVING CONTROLS

TUBULAR RADIATOR

DRIVERS SEAT

DRIVING CHAIN

10°

6'7"

12'9½"

MARK. V

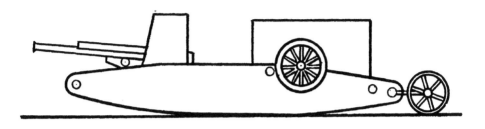

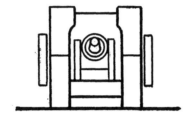

Gun Carrier.

Originally designed for carrying 60-pdr and 6-inch howitzers and
ammunition into action, these machines in 1918 were used chiefly for
transporting supplies across country. The tail-wheel was later discarded.

Opposite: Diagrammatic sketch of the Mark V, showing the internal layout.

Appendix 8

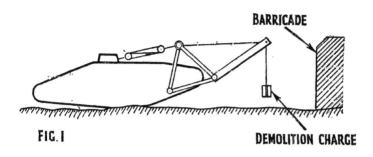

BARRICADE

FIG. I

DEMOLITION CHARGE

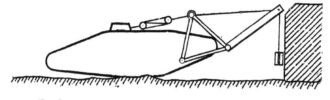

FIG. 2

DEMOLITION OF A BARRICADE

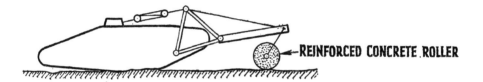

←REINFORCED CONCRETE ROLLER

FIG. 3   EXPLODING A MINEFIELD

Tanks were put to many additional uses during the war, apart from
fighting. Some of these are illustrated here. Figs 1 and 2 show how
anti-tank barricades or other obstacles such as debris blocking roads could
be destroyed. The demolition charge was held sufficiently far in front of the
tank so as not to damage the tank itself when exploded. The same principle
applied to clearing minefields (Fig 3); another method was by the use of
chain flails attached to a revolving drum. Figs 4 to 7 show a bridge crossing
device especially designed for tanks which enabled them to cross a 20-foot gap.
Throughout the fighting in the latter months of the war, the Germans made
considerable use of natural obstacles like small rivers and canals as a defence against
tanks. The Tank Bridge made it possible for tanks to cross such obstacles
even while under enemy fire. Larger sections could also be carried to form
100-foot pontoon bridges.

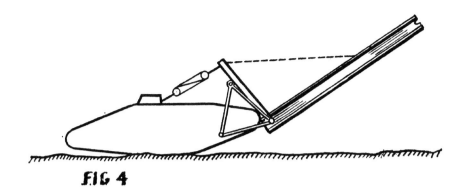

FIG 4

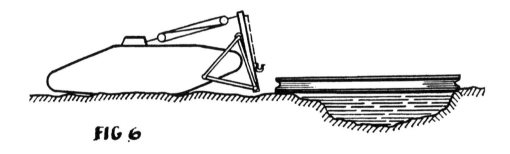

FIG 5

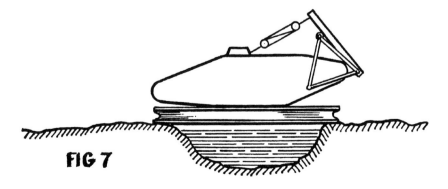

FIG 6

FIG 7

Data

Appendix 1

Length		Armament	
WITH TAIL	32ft 6in.	MALE	{ 2–6prs. 4 machine guns.
WITHOUT TAIL	26ft 5in.		
Width			{ 1 machine gun.
MALE	13ft 9in.	FEMALE	{ 4 Vickers light guns.
FEMALE	13ft 9in		
Height	8ft 0½in.	Engine	105hp Daimler.
Weight, equipped—		Maximum speed	3.7mph.
MALE	28 tons.	Average speed	2mph.
FEMALE	27 tons.	Approx radius	{ 6.2 hours.
Crew	Commander and	of action	{ 23.6 miles.
	7 men.	Trench crossing	
		capacity	11ft 6in.

Appendix 2

Length	26ft 5in.	Armament	
Width		MALE	{ 2–6prs. 4 Lewis guns.
MALE	13ft 6in.		
FEMALE	10ft 6in.	FEMALE	6 Lewis guns.
Height	8ft 2in.	Engine	105hp Daimler.
Weight, equipped		Maximum speed	3.7mph.
MALE	28 tons.	Average speed	2mph.
FEMALE	27 tons.	Approx radius	{ 9.5 hours.
Crew	Commander and	of action	{ 35 miles.
	7 men.	Trench crossing	
		capacity	10ft.

Appendix 3

Length	26ft 5in.	Armament	
Width		MALE	{ 2–6prs. 4 machine guns.
MALE	13ft 6in.		
FEMALE	10ft 6in.	FEMALE	6 machine guns.
Height	8ft 8in.	Engine	150hp Ricardo.
Weight, equipped		Maximum speed	4.6mph.
MALE	29 tons	Average speed	2.4mph.
FEMALE	28 tons.	Approx radius	{ 10 hours.
Crew	Commander and	of action	{ 45 miles.
	7 men.	Trench crossing	
		capacity	10ft.

Appendix 4

Length	32ft 5in.	Engine	150hp Ricardo.
Width		Maximum speed	4.6mph.
MALE	13ft 6in.	Average speed	2.4mph.
FEMALE	10ft 6in.	Approx radius of	⎧ 9.5 hours.
Height	8ft 8in.	action.	⎨ 40 miles.
Weight, equipped		Trench crossing	
MALE	33 tons.	capacity	13ft.
FEMALE	32 tons.		
Crew	Commander and 7 men.		
Armament			
MALE	⎧ 2–6prs. ⎨ 4 machine guns.		
FEMALE	6 machine guns.		

Appendix 5

Length	20ft.	Maximum speed	8.3mph.
Width	8ft 7in.	Average speed	5mph.
Height	9ft.	Approx radius	⎧ 10 hours.
Weight, equipped	14 tons.	of action	⎨ 80 miles.
Crew	Commander and 2 men.	Trench crossing capacity	7ft.
Armament	4 machine guns.		
Engine	2 Tyler, 45hp each.		

Appendix 7

Length, in fighting trim	43ft	Engine	105hp Daimler.
Width, in fighting trim	11ft.	Maximum speed	3.7mph.
Height, in fighting trim	9ft 4in.	Average speed	2mph.
Weight, in fighting trim	34 tons.	Approx radius of action	⎧ 11 hours. ⎨ 35 miles.
Crew	Commander and 3 men.	Trench crossing capacity	11ft 6in.